Fazil Iskander

RABBITS &
BOA CONSTRICTORS

Translated by Ronald E. Peterson

Ardis, Ann Arbor

Fazil Iskander, *Rabbits and Boa Constrictors*
Copyright © 1989 by Ardis Publishers
All rights reserved under International and Pan-American Copyright Conventions.
Printed in the United States of America

Ardis Publishers
2901 Heatherway
Ann Arbor, Michigan 48104

Library of Congress Cataloging in Publication Data

Iskander, Fazil'.
[Kroliki i udavy. English]
Rabbits and boa constrictors/Fazil Iskander : translated by Ronald E. Peterson.
p. cm.
Translation of Kroliki & udavy
ISBN 0-88233-557-X (alk. paper).
I. Title.
PG3482.S5K713   1989
891.73'44—dc20   89-17842
CIP

RABBITS &
BOA CONSTRICTORS

1

All this happened long, long ago in a land quite far to the south. To be brief, Africa.

On that hot summer day two boa constrictors lying on a large, moss-covered rock were warming themselves in the sun and peacefully digesting some rabbits they'd recently swallowed. One of them was an old, one-eyed boa, called Squinter by his fellow boas, though he was actually one-eyed and not squint-eyed.

The other was a very young boa who didn't have any nickname yet. But despite his youth, he was already rather skilled in swallowing rabbits, and because of that he inspired high hopes. In any case, although he had recently fed on mice and wild turkey chicks, he'd now taken up rabbits, which considering his age was a great success.

Dense tropical forests, with elephant-ears and coconut palms, banana and nut trees, stretched out around the resting boas. Butterflies as large as a small bird, and birds the size of a large butterfly flitted about. Parrots flew from tree to tree, flashing their colorful plumes, not even stopping to chatter in flight.

Occasionally branches cracked far up in the trees, and monkeys began to screech, upon which they heard the sleepy roar of a lion dozing nearby. Hearing the roar, they switched to whispers, but in a short time they'd forgotten about the lion and were screeching again, and once more the lion warned them that they were interfering with his sleep and that he had to go out hunting in the evening.

The monkeys reverted to whispering, but they just couldn't be completely silent. They were forever arguing about something, although it was hard to understand why, because they divided everything among themselves.

Yet the two boas resting on the mossy rock paid no attention to the screeching. Some nonsense, they thought, when they did catch the monkeys' racket—they didn't share some rotten banana, that's why they're arguing . . .

"There's one thing I can't understand," the young boa, the one who'd just recently learned to swallow rabbits, said, "why don't the rabbits run away when I look at them? After all, don't they usually hop very fast?"

"What's this — 'why'?" Squinter was surprised. "We simply hypnotize them."

"What do you mean 'hypnotize'?" the young boa asked.

We should say that in those distant times that we have undertaken to describe, boa constrictors did not smother their victims, but having encountered them, or rather having trapped them at rather short range, they caused them to freeze with just a look, and this is what the simple folk call hypnosis.

"Well, what is this hypnosis?" the young boa therefore asked.

"It's hard for me to answer precisely," said Squinter, although he wasn't squint-eyed but just one-eyed. "But, if you stare at a rabbit at close enough range, it's not supposed to move a muscle."

"But why isn't it supposed to move?" the young boa was a little surprised. "For instance, I feel it when they sometimes move in my stomach . . ."

"It's okay for them to move in your stomach," Squinter

agreed, "but only if they move in the right direction."

Just then Squinter fidgeted a little, in order to move along the rabbit he'd just swallowed, because it had suddenly stopped, as if it were listening to their conversation.

As a matter of fact, the old boa had experienced an unfortunate incident earlier in his life, after which he barely escaped alive and had lost one of his eyes. Every time that he remembered this incident, a rabbit would stop in his stomach and he'd have to fidget slightly to get it moving along again. The young boa's questions reminded him of that incident, which he didn't at all like to recall.

"I still don't understand," the young boa said after a while. "Why isn't a rabbit supposed to move when we stare at it?"

"Well, how can I explain it to you?" Squinter started to think. "Apparently, that's just the way life is arranged; apparently, it is such an ancient, and pleasant, custom . . ."

"It's pleasant for us of course," the young boa agreed, having thought about it a little. "But isn't it unpleasant for the rabbits?"

"Very likely," Squinter agreed, after a short pause.

Actually, Squinter was an extremely kind boa, although he wasn't kind enough to refuse to eat tender rabbit meat. He did the only thing he could for the rabbits,—he tried to swallow them in such a way that it caused them the least pain, and he ended up paying for it.

"But really, these rabbits," the young boa went on, "haven't they ever tried to revolt against this custom, which is so unpleasant for them?"

"There was an attempt," Squinter replied. "But it's best if you don't ask about it. It's not pleasant to remember . . ."

"The fact is," Squinter answered, "that it was one of my rabbits that revolted, and after that I was left with one eye."

"What did it do, scratch out your eye?" the young boa was astonished.

"Not exactly, but in any case, it was because of that rabbit that I have only one eye now," Squinter said, listening to try to find out what effect his words had on the rabbit's movements inside him. It was all right, it seemed that the rabbit was moving.

"Tell me," the young boa pleaded again. "I'd really like to find out how this happened . . ."

Squinter was quite an old and very lonely boa. The adult boas treated him with enmity or else ridiculed him; therefore he really valued the friendly relationship he'd developed with this young, but already skillful, boa.

"Okay," Squinter agreed. "I'll tell you, but just keep in mind that it's a secret; young boas aren't supposed to know about it."

"I'll never tell!" the young boa swore, and as all of us who take oaths do, he mistook the intensity of his curiosity for fiery loyalty to the vow.

"It happened about seventy years ago," Squinter began, "I wasn't much older than you then. On that day, I'd caught a rabbit at Asses' Pond, and I'd swallowed it in the usual way. At first everything went fine, but when the rabbit had moved to the middle of my stomach, it suddenly stood up on its hind legs, put its head against my spine, and . . ."

Right then Squinter broke off his story and began to listen for something.

"It put its head against your spine, and then what?" the young boa asked impatiently.

"It seems to me that someone's eavesdropping," Squinter said, turning his good eye toward the rhododendron bushes near where they were lying.

"No," the young boa protested, "it just seems that way because you don't hear very well. Tell me more!"

"I'm squint-eyed, not deaf," the old boa muttered, but gradually he calmed down . . . Evidently, he thought, I took the rustling of the breeze through the rhododendrons for the sound of an animal moving.

And he continued his amazing story. Now since he often interrupted his story, sometimes busying himself with the proper movement of the rabbit through his bowels, at other times suspecting that someone was overhearing what he was saying—which the young boa didn't agree with at all, because apprehensions about someone else's secret always seem exaggerated — we'll tell the story a little more quickly.

Because we aren't afraid of being overheard, and you'll agree that it's pleasant to be brave about someone else's secret, we'll tell everything as it was.

And so, Squinter, who was at that time neither old nor squint-eyed, had swallowed a rabbit by Asses' Pond. And truly everything was going smoothly at first, but then suddenly the rabbit got up on its hind legs and stuck its head into his spine from underneath, making it clear that it had no intention of going any farther.

"Hey, you," Squinter said to it, "think you're being cute? Move along, you have to be digested."

"But I've done this to spite you," the rabbit shouted from inside his stomach, "and I'm gonna stand here."

"Do something good with it after that," Squinter said, and having thought a little, added, "We'll see how long you can hold out . . ."

And he began to thrash about with his young, still elastic, and powerful tail. Lash, crash, but it hurt him more than the rabbit.

"Doesn't hurt me, doesn't hurt me!" it shouted from inside his stomach.

Actually, the boa thought, my skin's pretty thick, and all the pain intended for that miscreant is coming my way.

"Okay," Squinter said, still calmly, "now I'm going to pull you out of there."

He looked around and found a huge coconut palm, one of whose roots curved out over the ground because it had been washed clean by downpours. He carefully slithered under the root, up to the spot where his stomach was distended by that tenacious bunny rabbit.

"Lie down!" he shouted, "I'm gonna start pounding you now!"

"Go ahead and pound!" the violent rabbit replied from inside his stomach. "I'll push even harder!"

Then the boa got really mad and began to move with all his might under the root: Forward, back! Forward, back!

The palm tree shook and the coconuts fell to the ground, but that didn't bother the rabbit!

"Go on!" it shouted. "Again!" it screamed. "Not good enough!" it yelled.

The infuriated boa shook the palm so vigorously that one of the monkeys, who had been observing his strange behavior with some curiosity, unexpectedly fell on his head. The blow was quite perceptible, because the monkey had dropped from the very tip of the palm tree. Squinter tried to bite it, but after having landed smack on his head, the monkey had managed to jump off to the side. Squinter was going to dart after it, but the rabbit standing up in his stomach prevented him from stretching out.

Already mortified enough by the rabbit's behavior, and now totally dishonored by having a monkey fall on his head, the boa flew into such an incredible rage, and thrashed against the palm with such strength, that the root broke off. He banged his head against a nearby box-tree with all his might, and he lost consciousness.

He came to in about an hour, and having raised his head, he looked around. Although his head was still buzzing, he could hear the native hissing of his fellow boas around him. That means they found out, they've slithered over here, they're exchanging some remarks . . .

"If he's not lucky," one whispered, "he's going to choke on that rabbit . . ."

"And yet there are some animals who envy us," said one boa, who was known among his fellow boas for seeing everything in a gloomy light.

"Brothers," Squinter moaned, "has it been softened up in there, has it been squeezed along?"

"It's passed along about the width of a monkey's hand," one of the boas lying near him said.

"Depends on the kind of monkey," a marmoset suddenly said from high in the palm tree. "If you take an orangutan, then it looks like the rabbit didn't move more than a quarter of a hand . . ."

"That rabbit hasn't moved along, and it hasn't been softened up," chimed in the boa who was accustomed to seeing everything in a gloomy light.

"It's as straight as a stick, just like before . . ."

"Brothers," Squinter pleaded. "Help . . ."

"Things are looking bad for us," they suddenly heard the voice of the boa constrictors' Tsar, the Great Python. "A bad example is infectious . . . The monkeys are already starting to lecture us . . ."

"And why are the monkeys worse than any other animal?" the marmoset snapped peevishly from up in its palm tree. "Any little thing, and right away it's the monkeys this, the monkeys that . . ."

Hearing the Great Python's voice, poor Squinter was horrified, so much so that he even forgot about his own misfortunes.

The fact is that when the Great Python appeared among the boa constrictors, he uttered the battle hymn, to which all the boas listened, their heads raised as a sign of loyalty.

Here are the words to that short, but in its own way sufficiently expressive, anthem:

> Descendants of the Dragon,
> Glory's heirs, victors,
> Disciples of the Python,
> Young Boa Constrictors,
> Bear the sweet burden of rabbit ingested,
> This the future hath requested!

The Great Python considered all boas young, even the ones who were older than he. A boa who heard this greeting and didn't raise his head was thought to be a traitor and paid for it with his life.

And that's why Squinter, who hadn't yet become Squinter, was horrified to hear the Great Python's voice; after all, he had been in a state of unconsciousness and couldn't raise his head during the singing of the anthem.

But actually he needn't have been frightened. His habit of raising his head at the sound of the anthem was so ingrained that even in a state of unconsciousness when he heard the anthem, he had raised his head like all the other boas.

At the suggestion of the Great Python, the boas began to discuss how they could save their unfortunate tribesman. One boa suggested that he crawl to the top of the highest palm tree and crash to the ground, in order to squash the impudent rabbit.

"What are you talking about, brothers?" the suffering Squinter implored. "I couldn't possibly crawl up there right now . . . And even if I did, then I'd surely fall on the wrong spot . . . I'm not very lucky . . ."

"That's true, he wouldn't make it," the Great Python said. "What other proposals are there?"

"Well, maybe he could release the rabbit, and that'd be the end of it," one of the boas ventured uncertainly.

The Great Python pondered the proposal.

"On the one hand, that is a way out," he said, "but on the other, a boa's jaws constitute an entrance, not an exit . . ."

"But we won't let it go," the one who brought up this strange idea grew bolder, "as soon as it hops out, we'll work it over right away."

"I'd rather swallow a hedgehog than that rabid rabbit," said the boa who was accustomed to seeing everything in a gloomy light.

"Quiet," the Great Python warned them. "Whisper when you hiss; don't forget that there are enemies among us . . . In any case, inside one of us . . . In my whole life, and praise God I've reached the age of two hundred, there has been only one case of a rabbit hopping out of the mouth of a boa constrictor."

"Tell us," the boas began asking, "we've never heard about it."

"Brothers," Squinter began to moan, "please decide soon, or else I won't have enough strength to endure."

"Wait," the Great Python said, "let me speak with my people. It happened during the golden age, when there was a game especially popular among the boas—'Rabbit on rabbit, and on to the next.'"

"What was the game like?" the boas began to shout. "Tell us about it."

"Brothers," Squinter pleaded again, but no one was listening to him any more. Usually, if the Great Python began to reminisce about something in the past, it was hard to stop him.

But it seems there was such a game, which was popular among the boas in the olden times. It consisted of one boa (who had just swallowed a rabbit) finding another boa who had also swallowed one, and challenging him:

"Rabbit on rabbit, and on to the next?"

"You're on," the second boa replied, that is, if he agreed to play the game.

The game went like this: two players would lie next to each other. On the signal of a third boa, who took the role of referee, the rabbits would begin to race inside the boas—from head to tail and back. Whoever had the fastest rabbit won. It was easy to follow the rabbits racing inside because the boas' spines undulated freely to accommodate the rabbits' movements. What was amusing was that the rabbits raced because the referee, who had altered his voice, had shouted to the rabbits:

"Run, rabbits, there's a boa beside you!"

Then both rabbits began to scurry inside the boas, because once they'd come to after the hypnosis, they never remembered what had happened to them. They thought they'd fallen into some strange, dark burrow, and that they had to find a way out.

The boa whose rabbit was the fastest was declared the winner. And he collected his prize by having the loser find him another rabbit, hypnotize it, and modestly slither to the side, giving it to the winner to swallow. That was hellish torture. After two or three losses, some boas couldn't bear it and fell prey to nervous illnesses.

According to the Great Python, there was another feature of this game—whichever boa won most often saw his stomach stretched more and more, so much so that it was easier for the rabbit to course through it and, consequently, that boa had an even greater chance of winning. It turns out the boas even had one champion who had developed his stomach to the point where he used to cram a small goat inside him and force it to run.

"Tsar, uh, Tsar," a stubby boa suddenly interrupted the Great Python. This particular boa was known for his unceasing inquisitiveness, which had already led him to swallow bananas instead of rabbits, and he had even had the audacity to try and convince others that they were rather tasty. Fortunately, none of the other boas followed this example of free thinking. Nevertheless, the Great Python found Stubby unpleasant, almost a morally depraved freak.

"Tsar, uh, Tsar?" Stubby asked. "But what would happen if I, you know I'm short, and another boa, a longer one . . . Wouldn't a bunny be able to run faster from my head to my tail?"

"Ah-h-h, Stubby," the Great Python hissed at him. "You're always trying to set yourself apart. Don't think that boas were any less intelligent in the olden days than you are now. If one of the boas turned out to be longer, that longer portion was just twisted up."

Just then the boas got excited; they were in fact over-joyed and liked the Tsar's story so much, especially the amazingly fair conditions of this ancient game.

"Long live the Tsar, and his memory!" they shouted. "We want to play this remarkable game!"

"Unfortunately, it's not possible," the Great Python pronounced sadly, after he had waited for them to quiet down.

"Why?" the boas began to inquire dejectedly. "You're always trying to put limits on us! We also want rabbits to race inside us."

"Because a great catastrophe took place," the Tsar said. "And after that it was necessary to limit the freedom of rabbits to move inside boa constrictors."

"That's how it always is," muttered the boa who was accustomed to seeing everything in a gloomy light, "the rabbits' freedom is limited, and the boas suffer because of it."

"The fact is," the Great Python continued, "that during ing a game, one of the boas either opened his mouth too widely, or the rabbit got so worked up that it unexpectedly popped out of his mouth and fled into the forest."

"Unbelievable!" several boas exclaimed in unison.

"What a scoundrel!" others hissed and shook their heads.

"It's incredible, but it's a fact," the Great Python continued, "those were the darkest days of our history. It wasn't clear whether the fugitive rabbit would talk about our internal structure. Or how the other rabbits would accept his story. Measures were of course taken to capture it, a reward was announced, but demoralization had already spread to the ranks of the boas. And after a while, reports began to arrive, one after another, that this or that boa had caught the criminal and worked it over. But precisely because there was just one rabbit which had run away, and there were so many reports about it being swallowed, it was difficult to believe that it had indeed been caught.

"Then things gradually settled down. And anyway, we didn't notice any organized resistance on the part of the rabbits. It may have been that the rabbit was caught by some modest boa in some outlying area, who swallowed it without asking for a reward, not even aware of which rabbit he was swallowing. After a certain period, we punished the boa who'd gaped too widely, and life returned to normal. It is true that we had to ban this game as too reckless, and as an unnatural prolongation of a rabbit's life inside a boa. If you swallow one now, please go ahead and digest it. There's no need for any ceremony . . ."

The Great Python fell silent, recalling the magnificent details of how the careless boa had been punished. He really wanted someone to ask him about this punishment, but no one did, so he then whispered to one of his aides that he should organize just such a question from the ordinary boas in the audience.

"A group of boas is interested in knowing," the question finally rang out, "precisely how this gaping boa was punished."

"A most original question," the Great Python nodded. "It was a splendid spectacle . . . Now we've abolished this punishment, and I'll be honest with you: that was a mistake. The point of the punishment was to have the boa literally eat himself up. He wasn't allowed to eat anything for two whole months, and then his own tail was stuck into his mouth. It's difficult to imagine anything more instructive. On the one hand, he understands that it's his own tail and he is loath to swallow it, but on the other, being a boa constrictor, he can't help swallowing whatever comes into his mouth. By feeding on himself, he destroys himself; but by using himself for nourishment, he also prolongs his suffering. Finally, all that's left is the head, which the vultures and crows pick apart."

"What a frightful spectacle!" some of the boas exclaimed. And others squinted, glancing at their tails.

"One more worry we didn't need," said the boa who was accustomed to seeing everything in a gloomy light. "Now, if I curl up in a ring, I'm going to think about my tail accidentally slipping into my mouth."

"Be calm, though," the Great Python said, "since that time not one boa has ever released a rabbit."

"But still, it's preposterous!" Stubby suddenly shouted, though he wasn't sticking out too far from the distant ranks. The boas, however, didn't manage to say anything in response to that crude outburst, because they heard something that was totally unprecedented.

"Bastard!" they heard a voice say suddenly and distinctly. All the boas eyed each other suspiciously, trying to guess who had dared to utter that insulting word.

Squinter, who by then had been forgotten by everyone, realized with horror that it was the voice of the rabbit he had tried so unsuccessfully to swallow. He knew that he had to bear full responsibility for the rabbit's behavior and that thought filled him with terror.

Before the other boas guessed who had done the shouting, he began to look around, just in case, as if searching for the one who had insulted the Tsar.

"Who said bastards?" the Great Python hissed frightfully, looking through the ranks of his followers, who were hiding their heads in the grass, filled with embarrassment. "That wasn't you, was it, Stubby?"

"I was talking about an absurdity, not about a bastard," Stubby emphasized maliciously. "I wasn't talking about any bastard."

The Great Python had intentionally put the offending word into the plural, in order to insure that this insult, which could be applied to many boas, would relate to and include him only in the form of a general epithet, BASTARDS, directed at a large faction, at a general number of the boas present. It seemed to him that this part was less insulting, although basically any group contains within itself enough base material to far outstrip the quantity of baseness each member of the group would need to fulfill the norm in this area. That is, each bastard in that group could count on 150% of the norm for baseness, if they insisted on the mathematical expression of their measure of this highly unpleasant trait.

By the way, the natives later adopted the boas' custom of exchanging insults in the broad sense, in order to conceal their own measure of vileness (if we're talking about villains), or of baseness (as is the case here), when dealing with a bastard.

And so, Stubby had reminded him of precisely what had been said and the exact number that had been used by the unknown offender in his insult. And for just that reason, lest he direct more attention to that unpleasant detail, the Great Python stopped picking on Stubby so often.

"Ah-h-h, Stubby," he merely hissed in his direction, "I'm still gonna grind you into the dust."

"Bastard!" the rabbit in Squinter's stomach suddenly shouted again.

"Please be quiet, I beg you," Squinter hissed, growing cold with fright.

"I'm not here to be quiet!" the rabbit said loudly.

Nearby boas looked at Squinter in bewilderment, failing to understand how that misfortunate dared to speak with such fatal insolence. Because they had been carried away by the Great Python's tale, they had all forgotten about the lively, energetic rabbit sitting in his stomach.

"So . . . it was you?!" the Great Python hissed at last, turning to Squinter, who at that time still didn't squint, although he was now pretty close to becoming a squint-eyed boa constrictor.

" 'S not me, but what's inside me," Squinter hissed, horrified.

"A split personality?!" the Great Python suggested with disgust. This was considered a disgraceful illness among the boas.

"Oh, Tsar," Squinter pleaded, "you know you often forget when you're carried away by the glorious past, and you've forgotten there's a rabbit inside me."

"Well, what about it?" the Great Python interrupted him, "there's one inside me and inside others, too."

But right then one of his aides leaned over to him and whispered in his ear, reminding him of what had happened.

"Oh, right," the Tsar remembered, "so that was the one who called us all bastards."

"Yes, I did it!" the impudent rabbit exclaimed from inside the petrified boa. "You're the number one bastard, surrounded by your fellow bastards, and you're a nincompoop too!"

"I, I am a bastard?" the Great Python repeated, unable to find words because he was so angry.

"Yes, you. You're a bastard!" the impudent rabbit shouted with glee.

"I'm a nincompoop?" the Great Python repeated, scarcely able to believe his ears.

"Yep, you're a blockhead!" the rabbit screamed ecstatically. This time its voice was particularly distinct because poor Squinter had frozen, his jaw slack with horror.

An uneasy silence ensued; during this time the Great Python didn't take his eyes off Squinter.

"Your stomach has become a rabbit's soapbox," he said ominously, "but you'll pay for this, you miserable invalid."

"Oh, my Lord," poor Squinter pleaded.

"I'm not your Lord or your Tsar," the Great Python replied severely. "Any boa who harbors a talking rabbit is not the kind of boa we need."

"Nope, we don't," the boas hissed.

"Therefore," the Great Python continued, finally and decisively regaining his composure, "drag him over to Elephants' Path; let them stomp on that impudent rabbit, if this miserable invalid can't do the job himself."

Boas from the Great Python's guards seized Squinter and dragged him in the direction of Elephants' Path. While they were dragging him, the rabbit didn't stop shouting from inside his stomach, and at the top of its lungs to boot.

"Rabbits!" he shouted. "One rabbit escaped from the belly of a boa! The Tsar himself told about it! Resist the boa constrictors! Even in their stomachs, as I'm doing!"

"Hurry up, do it quicker!" the Great Python commanded, for he didn't at all like hearing this tribal secret divulged.

"We're trying," the guards replied, "but it's standing firm . . ."

"Brothers," Squinter whispered to them then, "have mercy, you know that the elephants will trample me along with the rabbit."

"You have no brothers but the rabbits," the guards shot back, pulling him into the depths of the jungle.

"Rabbits!" the impudent rabbit's voice still rang out, "one rabbit fled from the jaws of a boa! The Tsar said so himself!"

"Hee-hee-hee," someone suddenly began laughing spitefully. "Yeah, he said to keep their hissing to a whisper, and he divulged the tribe's secret himself."

"Degenerate," the Great Python replied, lest he demean himself by quarrelling with Stubby, "you feed on bananas, just like a monkey . . ."

"And how come you're so much better than the monkeys," a marmoset shouted, poking out from the dense crown of a nut tree. "Any little thing, and it's the monkeys this, the monkeys that . . ."

However, as soon as the Great Python lifted his head, it zipped back into the green crown and began to crack nuts, sometimes tossing the shells down angrily.

The monkeys maintained rather complex relations with the boa constrictors. As a matter of fact, the boas' customs did allow feeding on monkeys, but since they were so hairy and not very tasty, feeding on monkeys was considered poor form.

The Great Python expressed that point of view frequently, but the monkeys reacted ambivalently: on the one hand, they were interested in the boas' finding that they were unsavory, but on the other, they were painfully hurt by any remark about their imperfection. And that's how they lived, politicking on a small scale and tossing off individual insults at the boas. But at the same time they tried to retain the prevailing view among the boas — that they weren't tasty.

"Listen to this riddle," the Great Python said, having finally decided to disperse this mood caused by the impudent rabbit's screaming. "It's a joke too . . . When can a rabbit become a boa?"

The boas started to think. Some thought that the Tsar was trying to ferret out future traitors with the aid of this riddle, and so they decided to be quiet just in case he was doing that. Others offered more or less plausible suggestions. But of course none of them guessed the correct answer.

"The answer! The answer!" the boas began to shout.

"Fine," the Great Python said, "here's your answer: a rabbit that has been swallowed by a boa can become a boa."

"But how, Tsar?" the boas inquired.

"Because a rabbit processed and digested by a boa is thus tranformed into the boa. That means boas are actually rabbits at the highest stage of their development. In other words, we are former rabbits and they are future boa constrictors."

"Ha-ha-ha!" the boas laughed at the Great Python's joke. "We're former rabbits, well put!"

"All according to science," the Great Python added modestly, as if deflecting the boas' overly ecstatic gazes from himself personally.

"The Great Python is still truly a great python," the

boas said, slithering away and pleasurably recalling the Tsar's witticism. It was pleasant for them to feel that by swallowing rabbits, they were not only enjoying the rabbits' tender, delicate bodies, they were also turning the rabbits into themselves, as it were, raising the rabbits to their level.

"But what happened on Elephants' Path?"

Squinter could barely recall. All he could remember was the boas holding him until the elephants appeared close by. The rabbit never stopped yelling inside him, screaming that the rabbits had to struggle with the boas, even inside their stomachs.

He didn't recall if the rabbit had been able to hop out of his stomach when the elephants started to trample them: he had already lost consciousness before the first elephant stepped on him.

Two weeks later, when the rainy season had begun, he came to and found himself lying not far from Elephants' Path, where he had apparently been tossed by some finicky elephant's trunk.

His body had been trampled in several places, and now he had only one good eye, though he couldn't say whether the elephants had inadvertently crushed his eye, or that some bird had pecked it out later, when he lay unconscious. For some reason, this question bothered him tremendously, although he certainly had enough to worry about as it was. Squinter wished that somehow his eye had been crushed under the elephants' feet. And not pecked out by some vile bird that had taken him for a piece of carrion.

The thought that some bird had pecked out his eye like a seed gave him no peace, but finally his hunger pangs displaced this feeling. And several days passed like this, until a crow suddenly landed on him, attracted by his motionless pose. He was able to seize the crow when it perched on his head, intent on pecking his other eye out. From then on, actually for several months, he lay motionless, with his one good eye fixed on the sky. During that time he managed to catch several buzzards and crows, which had been tempted by his cadaverous pose.

And so Squinter survived, to the indifferent amazement of the other boas, and the evident displeasure of the Great Python. His fellow boas didn't touch him, but they did treat him with contempt, because as the Tsar had already said, any boa who harbored a talking rabbit was not the kind they needed.

Poor Squinter tried to cite examples of other rabbits that had been swallowed and then began to talk inside boas, but it didn't help.

"That's something totally different," he was told. "Those were just ravings under the influence of hypnosis. Your rabbit was doing it deliberately."

By the way, we forgot to mention that after the rabbit escaped from the boa's stomach, a law was introduced that rabbits should be digested immediately after swallowing. This law was more like a gentleman's agreement among the boas, because it was impossible to verify whether the boa had started to digest the rabbit right away, or whether he prolonged its life while extending his own pleasure.

In short, after all this happened, Squinter's fellow boas tried to avoid him. They didn't touch him, but they almost never spoke with him. Squinter suffered because of this, because every living creature has an ineradicable need to communicate with others like him.

For just that reason, and finding himself next to the young boa that day, Squinter had told him the whole, sad story. We should say, though, that he did conceal one point from the young boa, that even now he sometimes pretended to be dead so he could catch crows, because hunting rabbits with one eye was difficult, and his attempts at hypnosis frequently failed.

"By the way," the young boa asked, "how do you hunt with just one eye?"

"What can I do?" Squinter sighed. "I have to hypnotize them with my profile, and my eye gets tired."

"Now I've heard everything!" a rabbit's voice suddenly rang out.

"What?" Squinter said, his voice quivering. "Are you still alive? Did I swallow you again?"

"Not at all," the young boa set him straight. "That one hasn't been swallowed, it's over there in the bushes."

"Ooh," Squinter sighed. "I thought it was that one again."

"Well, so what did your hear?" the young boa asked, staring into the rhododendron bushes, trying to make out the rabbit there.

"I've been making observations about boa constrictors for a long time," the rabbit in the bushes said. "You have confirmed that the legend about the daring rabbit isn't a legend at all, but a true story. And once more my guesses have been correctly affirmed. Now I truly know that your hypnosis—is our fear. Our fear is your hypnosis."

"Are you taking advantage of us because we're both full now?" Squinter said, cocking an ear at his stomach.

"No," the rabbit replied. "This is the fruit of lengthy meditation and strictly scientific observations."

"Then why are you eavesdropping, if you're so smart?" Squinter asked, "or haven't you heard that it's dishonest?"

"I've also thought a lot about that," the rabbit replied, still not venturing forth from the bushes. "Eavesdropping in all cases is base. I know that. Even when you suspect someone of a crime, you shouldn't eavesdrop, because your suspicions might prove to be unfounded, but the method might take root. I mean, everyone who eavesdrops can say: 'I suspected him of having commited a crime.' But it's possible, and even necessary, to eavesdrop when you are absolutely certain that you are really dealing with a criminal. And you boa constrictors—you're murderers; you either commit murders or plan to commit them. Consequently, by knowing as much as possible about boas, I can give assistance to those rabbits still living."

"It seems that I might have heard something about you," the young boa recalled. "Are you the one they call Ponderer?"

"Yes, that's me," the rabbit replied.

"Well, come over here, if you're the one," the young boa said, feeling it was very likely that he could swallow a second rabbit.

"No," the rabbit responded. "I don't have the right just yet to take risks. Although there is no hypnosis, you could still bite me."

"Thanks for that," Squinter said, trying to give his entire story a slightly humorous inflection. Nonetheless, he had said many things that shouldn't have been picked up by a rabbit. All this smelled like new danger. And besides, Ponderer not only didn't stick his head out of the bushes, he set off then, rustling into the depths of the jungle.

"So, why don't you show yourself?" Squinter asked, even more wistfully.

"I want you to imagine that every rabbit you see could be Ponderer," the rabbit shouted back, his voice already blending into the background noise of the jungle.

Just then it seemed narrow and uncomfortable on that warm, moss-covered rock. Each boa thought it would be best to be rid of the other, who was a dangerous witness at best, but neither one summoned up the courage to attack. The young one because he feared he didn't have enough strength and agility.

"All this has turned out rather badly," the young boa hissed. "Most likely I'll have to denounce you before the Great Python for the way you slandered him here."

"Please don't," Squinter begged, "you know how much he dislikes me . . ."

"But what if this is discovered?" the young boa replied.

"We'll hope no one finds out," Squinter answered.

"That's fine for you," the young boa said, "you've already lived your life, but I have all of mine before me . . . No, I'll probably denounce you . . ."

"But then you'll probably suffer too."

"Oh, why is that?"

"Because I started to run off at the mouth, so you were obliged to rebuff me," Squinter reminded him about the age-old custom the boas had adopted.

As a matter of fact, the young boa thought, there is such a custom. He was perplexed. He couldn't figure out at all which alternative was more advantageous for him: to denounce Squinter or not.

"But what if this is discovered?" he asked pensively. "Well, okay, I'll keep quiet . . . And what will you do for me in exchange?"

"What can I do?" Squinter sighed. "I'm an old invalid . . . If you ever have any trouble catching rabbits, just play dead, and sooner or later a crow will land on your head . . ."

"To hell with your crows!" the young boa said indignantly. "Thank God I have rabbits regularly."

"Don't say that," Squinter replied. "Lots of things can happen in one's life . . ."

"Crows probably have tough meat?" the young boa suddenly asked.

"The meat's a little tough," Squinter agreed, "but if hard times come, it's better than nothing."

"But what if they find out?" the young boa again had doubts: slithering off the rock where they had been lying, he added, "Okay, I won't denounce you . . . It would have been better if I hadn't had anything to do with you . . . The Great Python was right a thousand times over when he said that a boa who'd harbor a talking rabbit isn't the kind of boa we need."

Slithering away from Squinter, the young boa still didn't know whether it was more advantageous to denounce him or not. Because he was young, he still hadn't realized that whoever ponders this question ultimately, and most certainly, goes ahead with the denunciation, because each thought aspires toward the accomplishment of the possibilities it contains.

That's what life is all about, Squinter thought. It would have been better if the elephants had crushed me, rather than live in an atmosphere of scorn and fear among my fellow boa constrictors.

That's what Squinter thought, but still, deep in his soul (which in a boa is located at the bottom of his stomach), he felt that he didn't want to give up on life. After all, it was nice and soft lying on this warm, mossy rock, so pleasant to feel the sun on his old rheumatic skin, while digesting a rabbit—why hide it!—this still gave him a good deal of pleasure.

2

On that same day, when the sun hung over the jungle, at about the height of a healthy baobab tree or a somewhat stunted larch, a special meeting of the rabbits had been called near the entrance to the King's palace on the Royal Meadow.

The King himself sat on a dias, together with his Queen. Over them waved the rabbits' banner with a picture of a cauliflower.

The banner's fabric was a large banana leaf on which a head of cauliflower, made of varicolored tropical flower petals, had been glued by using some pine pitch.

Actually, not one rabbit had ever seen a cauliflower. It's true that it was rumored among the rabbits (though it was sometimes necessary to reinforce these rumors) that the local NATIVES, together with some rabbits who had security clearance, worked on a hidden plantation; they were trying to raise cauliflower, and some success had been achieved. As soon as the experiments, which were close to being completed, could offer the possibility of planting cauliflower in gardens, the rabbits' life would be transformed into one continuous holiday of fertility and gluttony.

From time to time, the combination of colors in the picture of the cauliflower changed ever so slightly, and the rabbits saw this as a sign of the mysterious yet ceaseless work devoted to the betterment of conditions for the rabbits. Having noticed a slight change in the pattern of colors on the banner, they nodded to each other significantly, drawing for themselves optimistic and far-reaching conclusions. To speak about this aloud was considered indecorous and immodest; it was thought that these external signs of the inner workings of history appeared almost by accident, because of some kindhearted oversight on the part of the royal administration.

The rabbits lived in expectation of that happy time; they went about their normal lives, grazed in the jungle and savannah surrounding them, and they pilfered peas, beans, and ordinary cabbage from the gardens of the natives. The taste and high quality of the natives' cabbage in turn engendered dreams about cauliflower. And they brought this produce to the royal court.

"Well, how's the cabbage today?" the King used to ask when the rank and file rabbits rolled the heads of cabbage to him, thus meeting their garden tax, and then piled them up at the royal storehouse.

"Fine," the rabbits invariably replied, licking themselves.

"Well," the King said in that regard, "when we have cauliflower, you won't even want to look at this green stuff."

"Lord," the rabbits sighed when they heard this. "Will we really live to see that day?"

"Rest assured," the King nodded, "that we are keeping a close watch on the experiments and are assisting in any way we can . . ."

The great dream of having cauliflower helped the King to keep his multitude of rabbits in fairly compliant submission.

If the rabbits had any aspirations or yearnings that the King found objectionable, and if he couldn't put a stop to those yearnings in the usual way, the King in the last resort relied on his favorite means, and that of course meant invoking the name of cauliflower.

"Yes, yes," he would say to the rabbits in such situations, when he thought their ideas were unacceptable, "your aspirations are justified, but they're inopportune, because precisely at this moment, when the efforts to grow cauliflower are so close to fulfillment . . ."

If the rabbit who had the yearnings continued to be stubborn about them, he disappeared unexpectedly, and then the other rabbits came to the conclusion that he had been spirited away to the secret plantation. This was quite natural, since some of the best and smartest rabbits exhibited these tendencies, and these intelligent ones were of course needed most of all for the work on growing cauliflower.

If the family of the rabbit who had disappeared began to make inquiries about their departed relative, allusions were made to the relative now being "far away in that land where cauliflower grows."

And if the missing rabbit's family continued to be stubborn, they also disappeared, and then the rabbits said:

"Look at that, he's such a great scientist . . . They even allowed his family to join him . . ."

"Some people are just lucky," the females sighed.

No other suspicions arose in the minds of the ordinary rabbits because according to their vegetarian laws, punishment was permitted in the rabbit kingdom—hanging by the ears—but rabbits were never put to death.

And so, on that same day, which was fast drawing to an end, the King and his Queen were sitting on a dias on the Royal Meadow, the banner with the cauliflower insignia fluttering over their heads.

At a slightly lower level, were seated the courtiers (or, as the simple folk called them, those Admitted to the Table). And below them were seated the rabbits who aspired to be admitted to the table, and farther on the ordinary rabbits either stood or sat on the meadow.

It's not hard to guess that this special meeting of rabbits had been called because of Ponderer's extraordinary information.

"Our fear is their hypnosis! Their hypnosis is our fear!" the rank and file rabbits repeated, relishing that tempting thought.

"What a bold statement about this issue!" some exlaimed.

"And then ideas follow in quick succession," other rabbits waxed ecstatic, "just like peas in a pod."

"Oh, rabbits, just think what it'll be like!" still others said, they were so elated by Ponderer's great discovery that it seemed frightening.

And only Ponderer's wife, who stood in the crowd of triumphant rabbits, repeated from time to time:

"But why did my husband have to reveal the boas' secret? And where are those wise and educated rabbits Admitted to the Table? And what do we have to show for this? You know the boas will seek revenge on me and my little ones because of what he's gone and blurted out."

"You should be proud of him, silly," the rabbits around her said. "He's a great rabbit."

"Stop it, please!" she replied. "I know what kind of great rabbit he is! He's gone gray already and he still can't distinguish pea leaves from green bean leaves!"

Meanwhile, the King didn't like Ponderer's information one bit. He felt that this new twist didn't bode well for him. But as an experienced leader, an expert at judging the mood of the crowd, he watched the general celebration and didn't make any attempt to prevent it from spreading as far as possible. He understood that the crowd's celebration always reached a high point, after which it would almost certainly have to subside, and then it would be possible for him to express his own doubts.

In fact, when anyone, particularly a crowd, begins to celebrate, it isn't understood that sooner or later every celebration must die down. And then, when the mood does start to change, the person celebrating tends to blame the person who caused the celebration in the first place. He blames that person for the change in his own mood, because the instigator wasn't able to endow this celebration with an inexhaustible nature.

But if someone interrupted the universal celebration to express a critical attitude toward the object of celebration, then the crowd's anger would be directed especially strongly at him. After all, the celebrants thought that their festive mood would have no end, and this malicious, envious person had spoiled everything on purpose.

The King of the rabbits knew all this very well, and so he remained calm for a long time. And then when the celebrating was really dying down (though occasional flare-ups excited the crowd joyfully here and there), the rabbits began to notice that the King himself was silent for some reason. He was just quiet. His facial expression displayed the melancholic patience of a wise person observing the spectacle of universal delusion.

And then everyone noticed that the King had some doubts about the correctness of Ponderer's observations. The Admittees, who had noticed the King's doubts, whipped them up into overt indignation with their cries. The Admittees' indignation was then taken up by those Aspiring to be Admitted and turned to an expression of angry protest against the scientific rumors that had not been verified by the King.

Yes, the King was right when he sensed the tremendous danger inherent in Ponderer's words. All of the King's activities were tied to the fact that, together with his aides among the courtiers, he personally decided how much fear and caution the rabbits should experience when facing a boa, depending on the season, the atmospheric conditions in the jungle and many other factors.

And suddenly this cunning system for controlling the rabbits, which had been worked out over the course of years, was on the verge of collapse, because the rabbits, you see, didn't have to fear the hypnosis.

The King knew that by using hope (the cauliflower) and fear (the boa constrictors), he could direct the rabbits' lives in an orderly way. But you can't stay alive for long on cauliflower alone. The King understood this well, and so he gathered up all his wisdom about ruling and stepped out to face the rabbits.

"Rabbits," he began simply, "I'm an old King. I've been on the throne, praise God, for thirty years now, and I've never found myself in the jaws of a boa, and that must say something . . ."

"It means the other rabbits bring you everything you need to the palace!" one bold bunny exclaimed from the crowd.

It's true that it was now too dark to see who had been speaking. The Admittees and Aspirants hushed the rabbit who had dared to shout this as effectively as they could.

Looking at his courtiers, the King ordered them, in a stern voice, to bring enough lamps to light the area where his subjects were. Before that, there had only been some bubbles of transparent pitch, filled with fireflies, which had lit the entrance to the royal palace and the dias where the King and Queen were sitting.

"Oh, Sire," the courtiers reminded him in a whisper, shaking fireflies out of coconut shells, where they had been kept, and into the lamps, "after all, you yourself taught us how to be thrifty."

"Just as long as it's not at the expense of the regime's interest," the King replied under his breath, silently examing the crowd, while the courtiers fixed up the lamps at various places on the Royal Meadow.

"Rabbits," the King gently addressed his subjects, "before revealing Ponderer's mistake, I'd like to ask you several questions."

"Go ahead and ask," the rabbits shouted.

"Rabbits," the King's voice quivered, "do you like green beans?"

"And how," the rabbits answered in unison.

"And green peas, fresh ones, straight from the vine?"

"Don't say it, Sire," the rabbits moaned. "Don't awaken sweet memories."

"And what about cabbage?" the King thundered mercilessly. "I say, do you like to nibble on crisp, crinkly cabbage?"

"Oh-h-h," the rabbits began to wail and to inhale through their noses, making a whistling sound. "Don't aggravate us, Sire, don't pour sweet salt on the wound!"

"Well, if that's the case," the King continued, looking at the rabbits who had frozen in sentimental poses—munching on fresh pods, or nibbling on cabbage leaves, "then I'd like to address the main issue. Which one of us raises any peas, cabbage, or green beans?"

An astonished silence reigned for a short while.

"But, Sire," the rabbits began to shout, "the natives take care of that."

"That means the most perfect produce raised today (another quite refined hint about the cauliflower of days to come) belongs to them?"

"So it would seem," the rabbits replied.

"But how then," the King went on, "do you obtain this produce?"

"We steal it," the rabbits replied, crushed. "Didn't you know that?"

"Well, that's put a little too strongly," the King corrected them. "It's more appropriate to say that you remove the excess produce . . . After all, you do leave some for the natives, don't you?''

''We have to,'' the rabbits replied.

''Now I'd like to address the main issue,'' the King announced.

''You've already addressed the main issue,'' one of the rabbits shouted from the crowd.

''That was the first main issue, now for the second,'' the King didn't skip a beat: ''that boa constrictors swallow bunny rabbits—isn't that a horrible injustice?''

''Precisely,'' the rabbits shouted, ''that's what Ponderer's talking about.''

''Yes,'' the King went on. ''This is a most terrible injustice, from the rabbits' point of view. We try to fight against it with the only means we have available. But because of that horrible injustice, we take advantage of another tiny, but enchanting, injustice ourselves: appropriating the tenderest produce grown by the natives. Now let's say for the moment that Ponderer's right, although of course that hasn't been proved at all. But let's imagine that. It turns out that there's no hypnosis, so rabbits can hop wherever they want! Bravo, bravo, Ponderer! But then what happens? Then Ponderer will tell us, quote, 'If this most terrible injustice ever perpetrated on the rabbits ceases to exist, that means the rabbits must give up this pleasant (for us, of course) injustice in regard to the natives' gardens.''

''He won't say it! He won't say it!'' the rabbits shouted in unison.

''But how can you be sure?'' the King asked and turned to Ponderer, who was standing not far from the King and calmly listening to him. After he had spoken his piece about hypnosis, he had simply remained on the dias, because the King had ordered him to stay, so that on the one hand, no one would think the King was dissatisfied, and on the other, prolonged comtemplation of Ponderer made him appear more normal and thus less miraculous.

Ponderer was silent, although it was impossible to say, just by looking at him, that he was disturbed by the King's question.

"So what do you have to say to us?" the King again turned to him, trying to make him unmask himself now, before the other rabbits.

"I'll answer all the questions together, afterwards," Ponderer said calmly. "Let the King proceed."

"Fine," the King smiled ironically, although he was angry inside, and he was infuriated precisely because Ponderer had parried his blow—not as the result of a diplomatic move, but simply because of a stupid desire not to waste time on individual questions.

"We'll go on," the King continued. "Of course it's a terrible injustice that boa constrictors gobble up rabbits, and we're doing everything we can to decrease the number of victims. But why should we stress the dark side? Life is like that. And sometimes it offers us amazing gifts. For instance, say you bump into a boa, and you're terrified! But what happens? Perhaps it's Stubby, who's just stuffed himself full of bananas and doesn't even want to look at you. And again you bump into a boa! Once more you're terrified. But it turns out to be Squinter—and you're completely safe, because you happened to be on his blind side.

"Rabbits, brothers and sisters, we mustn't scorn these gifts of life! Remember that everything's connected in nature. So what if the most refined pleasure we receive from the holy trinity (peas, green beans, cabbage) is linked with the fear we feel when facing a boa? And what if, all of a sudden, without this fear, the most aromatic produce nature can provide would seem as tasteless and coarse as savannah grass?"

"That's horrible," the rabbits exclaimed. "Then it's not worth living."

"But if that's true," the King continued, warmed by his own rhetoric, "we'll stop dreaming about our future

Cauliflower. We'll stop experimenting and assisting in its development!''

"Horrible, horrible, horibble," the rabbits moaned; they were impressionable by their very nature, and the boas took advantage of that, as did the King himself, though we don't want to draw any parallels between them.

"Well, rabbits," the King continued, examining the crowd with an expression of penetrating wisdom, gained from experience. "We'll be candid, after all, we're among friends . . . Confess, when you return to your burrows in the evening and you find out from your mate that a boa has swallowed one of the rabbits, isn't it true that, along with the feeling of sadness about the brother who has perished, you also experience the comfort of safety in your burrow even more strongly? And the sweetness of licking your charming little bunnies' bodies? And embracing, cuddling (we're all adults here, I can speak frankly), snuggling up with your warm, affectionate mate?''

"Yes, yes," the rabbits replied, lowering their eyes, "it's shameful to admit it, but it's true . . .''

"There's nothing to be ashamed of, rabbits!" the King exclaimed. "You do experience these feelings together with the sadness for the fallen brother, don't you? Not separately?''

"That's it exactly," the rabbits replied, "everything's sort of mixed together somehow . . .''

"All the more!" a rabbit by the name of Sharpie shouted at the top of his lungs.

He was situated among those who Aspired to be Admitted to the Table. And now his audacious cry had been noticed by everyone; it was followed by a rather awkward silence. Actually, he had almost interrupted the King. The King frowned.

"All the more!" Sharpie again cried out, not at all disturbed by the universal attention.

"What 'All the more'?" the King finally asked him, sternly.

"All the more because of our ancestors," Sharpie exclaimed. "You see, if Ponderer's right, then it turns out that all our ancestors who perished heroically in the jaws of boa constrictors were simply fools and cowards, it means that they perished because of their stupidity!"

"A very apt remark," the King said, nodding his head and turning toward Ponderer. "I wonder how you'd answer this?"

"I'll respond to all the questions together," Ponderer calmly replied. "The King may continue . . ."

"Oh, you're so self-assured," the Queen couldn't restrain herself and sniffed scornfully at Ponderer.

"I've finished for now," the King said. "I could add only one thing: life is life. Since God created rabbits, then he must have had rabbits in mind!"

The conclusion of the King's speech was drowned out by friendly applause, praising the wonderful produce. From time to time the Admittees cried out, praising the King, and ecstatic whistles rang out from the Aspirants.

As always, rhythmic applause was offered to honor the great trinity, with certain private additions, among which the most frequently heard was—"Praise, too, for the lowly carrot!"

"It's interesting to note that each rabbit intended that his applause personally apply to the marvelous union of rabbits and produce. At the same time, he thought that others were not only applauding this union, but the King's speech as well. And since all of them thought that way, and each one gave some thought to admitting that the egotistical narrowness of his own applause was at least unattractive, they clapped for all they were worth, in order to conceal the egotistical narrowness of their own applause, and to merge with the common enthusiasm. They ultimately did, and they carried along this enthusiasm, because they were already in the grip of this current. So, little rockets of individual applause, flowing together, gave powerful might to the moving force of public opinion.

"Well, how'd you like the little speech?" the King asked the Queen, sitting down next to her and nodding at the ecstatic uproar among the rabbits.

"You were splendid, dear," the Queen said and delicately blotted the perspiration from the King's face with a cabbage leaf.

"Sharpie is enjoying some success," the King said and nodded in his direction.

The Queen smiled at Sharpie and motioned for him to come over to her. Sharpie hopped up quickly and then, facing her, he froze. The Queen smiled and gave him the cabbage leaf, which she had just used to wipe the King's face.

"You may eat it," she said to him. This was a sign of great favor, essentially the mark of being Admitted to the Table.

"Never!" Sharpie exclaimed fervently when he accepted the gift. "I'll dry it and preserve it in memory of your great and kind favor."

"As you wish," the Queen said and examined Sharpie with rather evident feminine curiosity. She liked his outward appearance, which was pleasant, and she liked his fiery, quick eyes. There was something in him that made her want to give birth to a little, quick-eyed bunny.

When all the tumult had died down, Ponderer, who had continued to stand before the crowd of his fellow rabbits, finally began to speak:

"I'll begin with the last point," he said. "As a rabbit, I feel there's no need to worry about the nature of the boa constrictor. Let them worry about their own nature . . ."

"But here he is worrying," Sharpie interjected spitefully. and looking at the Queen, he kissed the cabbage leaf. The Queen again smiled at him tenderly.

"That Sharpie," she said. "He's a real charmer."

"Consider him a permanent member of the Table," the King said, concentrating on the orator's words, and therefore forgetting that Sharpie had already received this favor.

The Queen thought about how much it was possible to do if a male didn't notice things because he was torn by social passions.

"Fine, let it be that way," Ponderer continued, "if a boa has the right to be concerned about its own nature, then a rabbit has the same right. And the very core of a rabbit's nature is that he doesn't want to be swallowed by a boa. I ask you, could we manage without boas?"

"Of course!" the rabbits exclaimed. "With pleasure!"

"Then tell me," the King leapt up, "why did God create boa constrictors?"

"I don't know," Ponderer replied. "Perhaps He was in a bad mood. But maybe He created boas so we could understand just what baseness means, just as He created cabbage, so we could know what bliss is."

"He's right!" the rabbits shouted. "A boa is base and cabbage is bliss!"

"Peas and green beans are also bliss," one of the rabbits reminded them, with such alarm in his voice that it seemed if he didn't remind them in time, then these wonderful delicacies would go out of fashion among the rabbits.

"I'd like to go on," Ponderer said. "And so, if God made the boas the way they are, then He made me the way I am. And if I sometimes ponder things, that means my nature as a rabbit tends to doubt. Thus, developing my nature as a doubter, which turns out to be a part of my existence, of my nature as a rabbit, has led me to look, listen, and think. Life, as our King tells us, is a great teacher. It and it alone has directed me to all of my current conclusions.

"Once, I found myself face to face with a boa. I felt the hypnosis binding my muscles. Terrified, I lost consciousness. But after a few moments, I came to and discovered, to my amazement, that I hadn't been swallowed, and that the tail of the boa which was rustling by had slithered on. I looked around and recognized Squinter, who hadn't noticed me as he slithered by because I was on his blind side.

And then a great thought started to light up, to take form in my mind. I understood that their hypnosis is our fear, and our fear is their hypnosis."

"Oh, holy naivete!" the King exclaimed, leaping up from his seat and addressing the crowd, "haven't I already spoken about the fortunate encounters with Stubby or Squinter?"

"Yes, you've told us," the rabbits replied, sensing there was something tempting in Ponderer's words, an inordinately alarming truth, but that the King's message contained the boring, but comforting truth.

"That's exactly it, rabbits!" Ponderer shouted fervently. "I experienced all the symptoms of hypnosis, but the boa hadn't even noticed me. That means I instilled this hypnosis in myself because of my fear."

"Brilliant!" one of the rabbits in the crowd exclaimed, thumped his forehead with his paw, and fell dead. His poor mind couldn't face that thought. A certain commotion arose in the crowd, but it didn't present any danger to breaking off the meeting. The convincing nature of Ponderer's example whipped the rabbits into a great celebratory mood, despite the loss of a rabbit.

"The first fruits of the new teachings!" Sharpie yelled, when they were carrying out the body of the rabbit who had died because of the force of his own revelation. But no one paid any attention to what he was saying.

"Magnificent! Magnificent! Magnificent!" the rabbits were chanting now, "Long live our liberator!"

"That still remains to be demonstrated!" the King shouted, hopping up and down. "Why is he so certain he hypnotized himself?! Only because Squinter passed by him on his blind side. Let my Scholar come forth and explain to Ponderer what happened, from a scientific point of view."

Then the rabbits gradually calmed down, and the Chief Scholar separated himself from the Admittees, waited for silence, and said:

"Of course Ponderer's information is not without some significant scholarly interest . . ."

The rabbits' reply to these words was rather enthusiastic buzzing.

"And although our little meeting is now running late," the Chief Scholar went on, "it's still too early to make any kind of conclusions. But what could have taken place during the supposed encounter between Ponderer and Squinter, or putting it into scientific language, a boa constrictor which is blind in one eye? Apparently, our esteemed colleague Ponderer, to our great fortune and common good, passed before the part of the boa constrictor's profile that is not able to form visual impressessions. For this reason alone, he remained alive, because the fatal hypnotic rays of its one working eye were directed away from our beloved colleague, which ultimately served as the basis for his truly frivolous conclusion in regard to hypnosis . . ."

"You know they keep all kinds of cripples around there," the King muttered, listening to the scholar and nodding in agreement.

"No, my dear rabbits," the Scholar continued, "hypnosis is still a fearsome weapon wielded by our enemies. Only by following the Multiplication Tables, worked out by our scholars (with the personal participation of the King), can we defeat the boas. Remember the Multiplication Tables, learn them, and the future of the rabbits will be worthy of Cauliflower!"

The Scholar's speech seemed convincing enough to the rabbits, but still the majority of them favored Ponderer's remarks.

By the way, the main point of the Multiplication Tables was that the rabbits would multiply more quickly than the boas, thus reducing the risk to each individual rabbit by having more rabbits than boas. According to the Tables, it followed that the chance of meeting a boa in the future would be diminished for each rabbit until it reached zero, and ultimately it would even pass that figure! Thus the rabbits liked multiplying very much.

But now the rabbits' mood was more sympathetic to Ponderer. Seeing this, the King decided to carry over the meeting to another, more auspicious time. With this aim in mind, and unnoticed by the crowd, he ordered the court illuminator to step forward.

"Rabbits," the latter said, "it's getting late. The lamps are going out, it's time to feed the fireflies."

"No problem," the rabbits yelled in response, "the forest is full of chunks of rotting wood. If we need some, we'll get it!"

The meeting was perforce continued, and again it was Ponderer's turn to speak.

"Rabbits," Ponderer said, "our Scholar, as usual, is talking nonsense! I contend that there is no hypnosis in general. Remember how many frogs there are at Frogs' Ford. Some boa or other swims across that ford every day. If a boa were able to hypnotize, then it would hypnotize dozens of frogs, whether it wanted to or not; the frogs would then be unconscious and would float up to the surface in front of it. And if the frogs had floated up, then waterfowl would fly after the boa swimming across. But as you can see, no bird ever follows a swimming boa."

"Exactly right!" the rabbits yelled. "There are hundreds of birds there, and not one ever flies after a boa."

"Ponderer's right!" they shouted. "Our fear is their hypnosis! Their hypnosis is our fear!"

While they were displaying their enthusiasm noisily, the King called one of the Admittees over to him, the one who occupied the position of Wise Old Rabbit.

The story of this rabbit's rise in stature, moreover, is not without interest. Near the King's palace, there was a tree which they called the carrot oak, because its acorns resembled carrots. Although the carrot oak's acorns aren't edible, the rabbits normally use them to decorate festive processions, and they consider this oak a sacred tree.

From time to time, carrot-shaped acorns (which are, incidently, rather heavy) fall from the tree. There have even been instances of serious maimings and rabbits being killed because they happened to be under one of these acorns falling from the tree's branches. And once this very rabbit happened to be under the carrot oak and sure enough, an acorn flew down and conked him on the head.

He had a brain concussion. And this was the first case of this type of illness in the rabbits' tribe.

"A brain concussion?" the King had been surprised by this unknown illness.

"Yes, a concussion," the doctors had affirmed.

"That means there was something to shake loose," the King had surmised.

"It means there was," the doctors had assented.

"When he recovers, we'll give him the post of Wise Old Rabbit," the King had decided, and when this ordinary rabbit did recover, he was immediately included among the group of rabbits Admitted to the Table.

"You're going to step forward and speak now," the King said to him, gloomily examining the crowd of rabbits, among whom he saw some who had raised their paws like fists, as if to threaten the boas.

"It seems to be all over," the Wise Old Rabbit said.

"You have to give it a try," the King said, at the same time giving orders to the chief of the royal palace guards to cover all the emergency exits in case there was any rioting.

"I'm an old, wise rabbit," the Wise Old Rabbit began, and he was partly right, because since he had received the post, he had managed to grow older.

"I swear by the carrot oak that made me wise that there is in Ponderer's words, . . ." but just then the rabbits' jubilation reached threatening proportions. It was even within the realm of possibility to expect the rabbits to depose the King and put Ponderer in his place.

"In Ponderer's words . . ." he repeated, letting a wave

of celebration pass by, "there is much that is true . . ."

"Hooray!" the rabbits shouted amicably, drowning out the screams of the Admittees, who could see no good in a coming coup.

And in the meantime, the Aspirants grew silent; in general they tried to make it appear that they never had any such aspirations. Some of them even got up and left their places, as if they were desperate to answer the call of nature. On the way back they were greatly delayed because they recognized old friends in the crowd and began conversing with them.

" . . . But in what the King said," the Wise Old Rabbit went on, "there is not much . . ."

The crowd of rabbits calmed down. The Wise Old Rabbit looked at the King and thought in horror: But what if they don't have a coup? When they were jubilant, the rabbits seemed stronger then the King, but when they fell silent, the King seemed stronger. And therefore he concluded rather unexpectedly (even for himself):

" . . . there is much that is true."

"So tell me, Ponderer," he continued, "if you're correct, and this terrible injustice against us is ended, will you still let us enjoy our divine trinity: green beans, peas, and cabbage?"

"Yes, yes," the rabbits shouted, "resolve our doubts!"

Ponderer silently looked out over his people and said nothing. Meanwhile the rank and file rabbits, having joined hands, began to stamp their feet, as they chanted:

"If you've permitted us to steal, then resolve our doubts! If you've permitted us to steal, then resolve our doubts!"

Ponderer remained silent. The King, who had been sitting gloomily, his head lowered, suddenly sensed a ticklish little ray of hope playing around his nostrils.

"Rabbits," Ponderer finally said, "I have offered to solve your greatest problem, by stating how we may stop fearing the boas. But as to what will come after that, I can only assume . . .''

"You see, he can only assume," the Queen exclaimed, and ripping a cabbage leaf angrily, she flung it aside. The Aspirants buzzed approvingly, trying to fix in their minds where the pieces of cabbage leaf had fallen.

"But he's still playing at being a teacher of life," the rabbit called Sharpie exclaimed. He had waited for a calmer moment to raise his voice and make it more easily distinguishable.

Ponderer rankled no one more than he did Sharpie, because when they had been young, they had been friends and often fell in love with the same females. Sharpie was certain that he could have made as brilliant a discovery as Ponderer, if he hadn't aspired to be Admitted to the Table. Because he was bogged down in the philosophy of his own existence, he couldn't find any time at all for busying himself with the existence of all the rabbits.

"It's fine for him," he used to say to his acquaintances, when the talk turned to Ponderer, "you know he's not trying to be Admitted."

"But who's stopping you? You don't have to aspire to be Admitted," his acquaintances asked him at those times.

"It'd be better if you asked who's helping me," Sharpie would answer them, deliberating about how he could be more visible in the King's presence. In the meantime, Ponderer continued:

"Rabbits," he said, "if we try at the very beginning to see the very end, we'll never make any progress. It's important to make the first step, and it's important to be certain that it be the right one."

"Well, at least tell us one thing," the rabbits shouted. "Tell us what you think about the green beans, the peas and cabbage . . ."

"I think," Ponderer said, "when this terrible injustice perpetrated on us is banished, we must give some thought to our unjustified attitude toward the natives' gardens.''

"Oo-oo-ooh!" the rabbits wailed, dissatisfied. And the King shook his head too, as if to say: Just listen to him, he'll fix you up with a nice, happy life.

"Actually, the important thing isn't getting rid of all this wonderful produce," Ponderer said, "but learning how to raise it ourselves."

"Oo-oo-oh," the rabbits wailed in unison. "Bor-ing . . . But how will we till the soil?"

"I don't know," Ponderer said. "Perhaps we could work something out with the moles, maybe something else . . .''

"Oo-oo-ooh," the rabbits wailed, even more anguished. "What if the moles don't agree? That means good-bye green beans, and peas, and cabbage!"

And then a simple rabbit, whom everyone respected, stepped forth on behalf of the ordinary rabbits.

"Listen, Ponderer," he said, "we all like you, you're our guy, you think about us. And that's fine. But you haven't thought everything out. Take me, for instance, I go out into the forest, to the savannah every day. I visit the natives' gardens . . . I could run into a boa on any day, or I might not meet one. Day before yesterday, for instance, I didn't run into one, yesterday either, and today, thank God, as you can see, I came back alive and well.

"So what happens? I can go to the natives' gardens every day, but a boa couldn't pos-sib-ly swallow me every day. So that means I win. You haven't thought this all out, Ponderer. Why don't you go back to your green hill and think up something to keep the boas from bothering us and to let us have our produce. God likes things in three, as they say. Then all of us will unite and follow you."

"That's right! That's right!" the ordinary rabbits began to shout, because the rabbits' favorite way of deciding was not to make a decision at a difficult moment.

"I'll personally be the first to follow you!" the King shouted, "as soon as your conclusions are confirmed!"

"Long live our noble King!" the rabbits shouted, satisfied with their decision not to make any decision.

"And, what's more," the King continued, "So that Ponderer will not be distracted, his family will receive, from our own table, two carrots at full value!"

"Long live the King and his generosity!" the rabbits yelled.

"To multiply and forge ahead — that's our weapon!" the King shouted, and to show that the meeting was over, he took the Queen's paw and together they retreated into the palace.

The rabbits also called out to others walking nearby and dispersed to their own burrows. Some of them, feeling the pangs of conscience, warmly praised Ponderer's remarkable idea, although they also pointed to its immaturity.

Some of the rabbits asked Ponderer's wife if she were content with the royal assistance.

"Goodness knows what it'll be like, but at least it's something," she replied to the inquisitive rabbits, and then she tried to find out if today were included in the terms of the announcement and if she could therefore count on receiving four carrots the next day from the royal treasurer, who was known for his stinginess and chicanery.

"Today's included!" the rabbits replied with totally liberal decisiveness, and each one answered more liberally and decisively, in order to make up for the lack of decisiveness in supporting her husband during the meeting.

Ponderer sat sadly on the now deserted Royal Meadow. Only one young bunny remained by him, and this one not only believed in the correctness of his teachings (actually, there were a lot of them who did), but he'd decided to risk his calm, peaceful life and follow him.

"What do we do now?" he asked Ponderer.

"There's nothing to do," Ponderer replied. "We'll think some more."

"Maybe I could think along with you?" the young rabbit asked, "since the time I first heard what you were talking about, I've had this yearning to know the truth."

"We'll think together, Yearner," Ponderer said. "I've used up all my mental energy studying the boas, but I didn't realize that my fellow rabbits weren't prepared to live up to the truth."

3

The next morning, the rabbits' life returned to normal. Some grazed on the savannah, others preferred the shady jungle, and a few set off for the natives' gardens.

Ponderer had been sitting on his green hill since the morning began, this was where he had earlier contemplated his observations of the boas. But now his pondering about the predators had been expanded to include worried thoughts about his fellow rabbits.

There was a marvellous view from the hill, down over the savannah, to a bend in the river where the water spread out for some distance, and so the jungle's inhabitants called it Frogs' Ford.

Yearner had been grazing on the slope of this green hill that morning, glancing from time to time at Ponderer and trying to determine, from the other rabbit's pose, whether he had thought of anything new or not. After a while, his intellectual curiosity overcame his appetite, and without finishing his breakfast, he climbed up to the top of the green hill.

At that same time, a hearty breakfast (in honor of the previous day's victory) was being held in the spacious dining room at the royal palace. All the rabbits Admitted to the Table were of course sitting at the table. The King was in a fine mood, he joked a lot during the meal, and occasionally he raised a bamboo goblet that was filled with coconut wine. The Admittees also quickly filled their own goblets and drank that merry, bracing beverage with their King.

It's interesting to note that several guards were sitting among the Admittees. Seeming to be Admittees themselves, they kept track of the conversations among the true Admittees, in order to discover in time any traces of a conspiracy, or simply any deviations from the King's line, which later might possibly lead to a conspiracy.

But since they were in fact not Admittees, even though they sat there as Admittees, they had been instructed not to overdo it, particularly with the valuable produce, such as cabbage, green beans and peas. But since the Admittees were aware that guards mingled among them, as Admittees, and they also knew the guards were not permitted to eat as much as the true Admittees, they looked around to see how much the other Admittees were eating, and at the same time they tried to the best of their ability not to be taken for spies, as the simple folk called them. But since those who were commonly called spies knew that if they were too modest about their portions, the others would discover their true function at the table, they blended in by eating as much as possible, which in fact agreed with their natural inclinations.

This time there was one rabbit missing from the ranks of the Admittees, the rabbit who occupied the position of Wise Old Rabbit. The King, of course, had not failed to notice his vacillation the previous day, and in his place sat Sharpie, who proposed that the Wise Old Rabbit be rechristened Wiseole, a proposal that was greeted by lively approval. Apropos of this proposal, the King told several anecdotes from Wiseole's life.

When the breakfast was in full swing, the rabbit everyone was now laughing at, who just yesterday had been considered the King's closest advisor, came into the dining hall, picking his teeth, which had been worn down over time. It seemed that he now took his breakfast in the kitchen. And just then the King mockingly suggested that his former sage be placed under the carrot oak's branches, to wait and see if a carrot-shaped acorn would fall on his head. Then they could find out whether or not he'd have another brain concussion. All the Admittees laughed at the King's joke and assured him that now there was nothing inside to shake loose.

"I know," the old rabbit said, "why I've been moved to the kitchen, but I don't know why the vegetables I've been given aren't very fresh."

"What, what," the King inquired, winking to the rabbits around the table, "the vegetables are . . . not very . . . very fresh?"

The Admittees began to roar with laughter, some of them falling from the table with that affectionate trustfulness, known to lovers in similar situations, when they sink into their lover's arms, often combining this movement with a fleeting caress. In this case, the rabbits happened to snatch a little bit of cabbage leaf or a pod of fresh peas while they were falling, which to them meant the same as a lover's fleeting caress.

"I swear by the carrot oak that made me wise," he said, "I made a little slip when I was talking. But didn't I correct my mistake later?"

"You bet," the King responded, smiling. "Otherwise you wouldn't be eating in the kitchen, but somewhere else much farther away. Well, okay, sit down here. I'm a kind King. But the next time, you'll know who furnishes the vitamins for your not very . . . very sharp mind."

Thus the Wise Old Rabbit was brought back to the table, and everyone was in a good mood. It's true that the King kept the joking name, Wiseole, for him, which on the one hand brought a certain jocular ambiguity to his position, and on the other, nudged Sharpie even closer to the royal family.

For approximately one month, Sharpie lived among the

Admittees to the Table, without a care, consuming the best royal drinks, not to speak of the very freshest vegetables, obtained from the natives' gardens.

Sharpie liked everything there, and only one thing surprised him: when the rabbits Admitted to the Table gathered, for some reason neither the King nor the others ever spoke about cauliflower. That was very strange, because every time the King met with the ordinary rabbits, the question of cauliflower arose in one fashion or another. But here, evidently, speaking about it wasn't considered good form.

When he pondered this, he decided that there was probably an even smaller circle of intimates — those Admitted to the Smaller Table — among the regular Admittees, and they probably not only talked about it, they must even try it once a week. That's what Sharpie thought, but he didn't have the courage to ask anyone, because he didn't know who among the Admittees belonged to this smaller circle. And Sharpie thought by asking he would be confessing that he was not a member of this more elite group. So he decided to wait for a more suitable occasion and ask the King about all this.

And such an occasion did arise, because the King once asked him to stay behind with him after lunch, for a personal conversation.

"I have a mission for you, of national significance," the King said. He waited for the Queen to close the door, and when she had returned and sat down next to Sharpie, he added, "Are you prepared to carry it out?"

"Oh, Sire," Sharpie said, lowering his eyes.

"Our court Poet here has jotted down some verse. So, what I want you to do is go out into the jungle, to the Neutral Path, and sing this verse along it, there and back . . ."

"My ears are at your service," Sharpie said, wiggling his ears.

The King attentively examined his ears, as if trying to determine how reliable they actually were.

"Then listen," the King said. And he read the poem, which had been written down on a broad banana leaf, using elderberry juice:

> A pondering rabbit
> Sits upon a little hill
> And watches the savannah,
> From there he sees Frogs' Ford,
> But a storm is fast approaching!

Sharpie's heart skipped a beat when he realized what this terrifying riddle meant.

"Your majesty," he said, quivering, "doesn't this mean . . ."

"It doesn't mean that a bit," the King interrupted him, frowning.

Sharpie understood immediately that by singing this verse, he would be abandoning his fellow rabbit to the boas. And he immediately decided to give up his position at the royal table and return to the ranks of the ordinary rabbits. After all, he wasn't evil by nature, even though he was ambitious. But this was a very ticklish point. According to the ethical system adopted by the court, a rabbit who was demoted in rank was obliged to return all the awards he had received from the King.

It would mean that he'd have to give back the cabbage leaf the Queen had once given him, and which had begun his advancement. But as a matter of fact, he had been so overjoyed that he had eaten half the cabbage leaf, although he wasn't supposed to have eaten it all all, for he himself had promised to dry it and turn it into a keepsake.

The fact is that he had the right to eat a cabbage leaf given to him by the Queen in the form of a present, as she herself had suggested; but he had elevated this present to the level of an award, as he had suggested, and so he then had no right to eat it.

All of this flashed through Sharpie's mind as quickly as lightning, and he understood that it would be awkward, that in fact there was no way he could return this half-dishonored cabbage leaf right now. Of course he understood that no one would persecute him for this, but rabbits were inclined to think that today's awkwardness was less bearable than tomorrow's treachery. Awkwardness — this is right now; but tomorrow — that's then, who knows what'll happen. Maybe nothing will happen, or, let's say, there'll be a solar eclipse and all bets will be off because of that.

"Okay," Sharpie said, shuddering and looking like a martyr before the King, "could I ask for one change though?"

"If it doesn't alter the main point," the King agreed.

"I'd like to sing it this way," Sharpie said and then sang:

> A pondering someone
> Sits upon a little hill
> And watches the savannah,
> From there he sees Frogs' Ford,
> But a storm is fast approaching!

"Sounds fine!" the King said and gladly slapped Sharpie on the shoulder. He understood that Sharpie was trying to outwit him and at the same time he had rather successfully outwitted his own conscience.

" . . . It's even better," the King added, "because some might think this verse is full of prejudice . . ."

"Well, then could I perhaps add just one more change?" Sharpie requested. And without even waiting for the King to agree, he quickly sang:

> A pondering someone
> Sits upon a little hill.
> Sa-va, Sa-va, Savannah!
> And Fro-go-ro-go Ford!
> But a storm is fast approaching!

"Well, that really is a song without words," the King waved his paw. "That means giving him lots of slack."

"It's okay, it's okay," the Queen suddenly interrupted him, "this way it's more alluring. I have only one request. Please, when you sing it, put as much emphasis as you can on the last syllable in the third line: 'Sa-va, Sa-va, Savann-POW!' SavanNAH, all right?"

"Of course," Sharpie said, "I'll most certainly keep that in mind."

"Okay," the King said, "that's how it'll be. Just change it slightly, to 'A view, savannah, ka-POW!' and we won't haggle any more."

"Fine, Your Majesty," Sharpie said.

"And Fro-go-ro-go Ford, you say?" the King asked, trying this line out loud.

"Perfectly correct," Sharpie affirmed. "I sing: 'And Fro-go-ro-go Ford' . . .''

"In our parts," the King said, lost in thought, "there are three well-known fords: Tigers', Apes', and Fro-go-ro-go . . . You don't think there will be any confusion?"

"Of course not," the Queen said. "You shouldn't think they're dumber than we are."

"My Lord," Sharpie asked, "there's just one thing I don't understand. Why does it have this line: 'But a storm is fast approaching'?"

"Oh, you know our Poet," the King said, "he just can't get by without his storms . . .''

"Does he know how his verses are being used?" Sharpie asked. It was easier for him if he wasn't the only one participating in Ponderer's betrayal.

"No, of course he doesn't," the King wrinkled his nose. "He's a poet, he's always got his head in the clouds. Why should he be let in on all these unpleasant earthly matters?"

"Yes, of course," Sharpie sadly agreed.

"Okay," the King said. "The text has been tampered with for the last time. I'm surprised at how quickly you were able to remove some naturalistic details . . ."

"Oh, Sire," Sharpie lowered his eyes, "in such cases, these things just have a way of working out . . ."

"By the way," the King recalled slyly. "You can finish eating the little cabbage leaf the Queen gave you."

"Oh, my Queen," Sharpie whispered, hiding his head between his paws, terribly embarrassed, "forgive this . . . weakness."

"What's there to be embarrassed about?" the King cheered him up good-naturedly. "We're all rabbits . . . But do you see how good our information service is, eh, Queen?"

"Oh, you little scamp," the Queen said and shook her paw in sad reproach at Sharpie. "You should have seen, my King, the genuine fervor in his eyes when he shouted: 'Never!' "

Then the Queen gave Sharpie the royal journal, where it was written that on such-and-such a day, a courtier named Sharpie was to sing the variation on the "Stormy Petrel" march, without words, so that all the residents of the jungle would know that the rabbits were hale and hearty and were cheerfully multiplying.

Sharpie signed, and the King personally patted him on the shoulder.

"Now you may ask," the King said, "for anything you might like, for anything I might be able to do."

"There's just one thing I'd like to ask," Sharpie replied. "I'm surprised that no one ever mentions cauliflower at the royal table, though you and the others often recall it when you're conversing with the commoners."

"What's there to say?" the King shrugged. "The experiments are being conducted successfully and we're helping in any way we can . . . All the lily-livered little rabbits think that in addition to the Admittees to the Table, there is an elite, admitted to a more intimate table."

"You mean there isn't?" Sharpie asked, downcast.

"No, my dear rabbit," the King replied, giving him a friendly little hug. "There's nothing more I can allow you into, except the conjugal bed."

"Oh, King, how coarse you are," the Queen said and turned away, at the same time quickly glancing over at Sharpie.

But Sharpie was so crestfallen that he didn't even notice this glance.

"Now do you understand," the King said to him, "why I have the hardest time of all?"

"No," Sharpie said, quite distressed that this elite didn't exist.

"Because for each of us," the King replied, "there is a secret, there is something to aspire to. I have no secret in regard to comprehending. If I don't understand something, then this condition remains forever . . . That's why it's the most difficult for me, in my kingdom . . . But I have one consolation. It's even harder (the King pointed with his paw toward heaven) for Him . . ."

"But if there's no elite among those Admitted to the Table, then there's nothing for me to strive for!" Sharpie exclaimed, understanding the King's sadness through his own disappointment, "and how sad that is!"

"It'll pass," the King said with assurance. "With time the aspiration to remain at the Table becomes the only unquenchable desire of the Admittees. And now, go . . . Get plenty of rest . . . So tomorrow you can go out to the Neutral Path with fresh vigor . . ."

Sharpie bowed and left the royal palace.

"You know what I like about Sharpie?" the King said,

walking around his study. "That he has a conscience."

"Since when?" the Queen asked, somewhat surprised.

"You don't understand anything," the King said, stopping in the middle of his study. "When you give a rabbit a delicate mission, a less than fatal dose of conscience can come in handy."

"Now I really don't understand you," the Queen replied absentmindedly, because she was still annoyed that Sharpie, with his lively little eyes, had turned out to be so unreliable. He betrayed not only me, the Queen thought, but also his enchanting eyes...He essentially betrayed us...

"Yes," the King repeated, continuing to stroll around his study, "when a rabbit experiences a certain shame while carrying out a delicate mission, he tries to do it as cleanly as possible, lest he be carried away with shame if he leaves some untidy clues behind. And this is exactly what we need. A non-fatal dose of conscience, that's what our wise men should innoculate the rabbits with."

"But look what kind of men we have," the Queen said, and sighed. "He said it himself: 'Never!' and he went ahead and ate it."

"Let's hope he eats it up," the King replied, somewhat vacantly, because he was thinking about how best to inculcate this non-fatal dose of conscience in the rabbits, so that they wouldn't leave behind any untidy clues when they were working for the good of the kingdom.

4

Now we're going to divert our attention from the plot and tell a story about how the Poet and the King of the rabbits got along.

The Poet's character combined, in a rather odd way,

the most sincere sympathy for all kinds of grief and a romantic ecstasy about all kinds of storms, both in nature and in people's lives.

By the way, the King had come to power thanks to one of these storms, which the Poet unceasingly praised.

"This isn't exactly the storm I was calling for," the Poet used to say at first, dissatisfied with the King's reign.

But then they settled their differences. The King tempted him, promising him that praising storms would be made the indivisible, single, and complete content of the rabbits' intellectual lives. The Poet couldn't hold out against that.

In short, the Poet terribly loved to sing the praises of stormy petrels and felt just the opposite about contemplating harbingers of misfortune.

If he saw a stormy petrel — he rejoiced. If he saw a harbinger of misfortune — he grieved. He did both with total sincerity and could never understand that praising stormy petrels most assuredly led to the arrival of harbingers of misfortune.

It sometimes happened that he didn't have a chance to cry his fill on the harbinger's shoulder before he caught sight of a stormy petrel rising into the sky over the drooping shoulder, and he'd greet the bellicose bird with the joyous shout:

"Let a storm burst forth over the world!"

He was certain that his poetic voice would embolden the stormy petrel and remind the rabbits all round that in addition to their love for fresh vegetables, they had a higher destiny — a love for storms. The rabbits sometimes overheard him speaking, comparing the love for vegetables to the love for the higher destiny, and every time they were amazed because they clearly felt this love for vegetables in their souls, but the love for the higher destiny they felt only vaguely, — actually they didn't feel it at all.

Because of his advanced years, the Poet still rejoiced

at the sight of a stormy petrel, but due to his weaker eyesight, he sometimes mistook ordinary crows for stormy petrels.

And the King, who didn't want the Poet to seem confused in front of the ordinary rabbits, ordered a sharp-eyed guide rabbit to accompany him, in order to stop him in time. By the way, this guide bunny also protected the Poet from falling into pits and traps when they were strolling in the savannah, because the Poet always gazed up at the sky, searching for stormy petrels, and he never noticed anything around him.

"Let a storm . . . " the Poet would say, but then the sharp-eyed guide rabbit would interrupt him.

"Uncle Poet, that's not a stormy petrel, that's a crow!"

"Oh, a crow," the Poet responded, somewhat disappointed. "Well, that's all right, calling a storm never hurt anything."

But we've disgressed again, and we should be talking about the lives of the Poet and the King in an orderly way. Besides, this whole story is basically much sadder, and we really should tone it down correspondingly.

In short, when the King and the Poet had made peace, the King promised to introduce — in the immediate future, right away — universal education among the rabbits.

"Only in this way will my wise commands and your divine verse be accessible to all rabbits," the future King used to say.

But it turned out that the day-to-day life of a King is filled with such a great quantity of trivial matters of state that the King never got to any of his major projects.

"You spin around the throne like a squirrel in a cage," the King used to say when his friend from their younger days reminded him about his bold plans. "But I've ordered ten more tubs of ink to be prepared. So something is being done in that regard."

The King stored up elderberry ink, so that when the

time came, the whole kingdom could be supplied immediately with the means to fight illiteracy. But time passed and the King was never able to get around to dealing with universal education for the rabbits. The only thing he was able to do, from time to time, was to give orders to prepare several more tubs of elderberry juice in the event it might be needed in the future.

But the time when it might be needed never came, and the elderberry juice fermented in the tubs, turning into a marvellous, strong drink, which no one had any idea about, however, until the Poet happened to be chewing dejectedly on his poetic quill many years later and he accidentally sucked some of the invigorating juice through its hollow stem. The rumor about the ink's properties spread like wildfire among the rabbits, and they began to display an unquenchable thirst for self-education. But we'll talk more about that another time.

Though he had maximum power as ruler, the King of the rabbits realized bitterly that all his efforts were being expended on staying in power. What is power for, the King sometimes thought, if all my efforts are devoted to staying in power? Finally he came to the conclusion that he had to augment the royal guard, in order to free up some time and strength for those matters which were the goal of his striving for power.

And so he increased the size of the royal guard and felt that things were getting better for him: a part of his effort which had been devoted to staying in power was now freed up. But one fine day the perfectly commonsensical idea occurred to him that such a powerful guard could itself try to wrest power from him. What should he do about this?

If he were suddenly to decrease the size of the guard, the King decided, those rabbits with evil intentions would think that the appropriate moment had come for them to seize power. Thus he made the guard even larger, and he gave these new guards the secret assignment of protecting the King from the older guards.

But this made the King's situation even more complicated. It became clear that the new guard, which had these powers in respect to the old guard, would not be closely supervised and therefore would be a danger to the King. So then he gave the old guard a secret order to keep track of the new guard, in the event that the new ones would want to betray him.

But that confused the King even more and made his life more complicated. By having such an enormous guard with complex lines of authority meant he had to give each guard a daily work assignment personally, otherwise, one of them might be corrupted by irresponsible power and become a plotter.

And so, in order that each member of the guard had work, work he would have to give an account of, the King had to initiate surveillance over the whole nation of rabbits, especially those rabbits who served the King in an official capacity. But the King had absolute trust in many of the rabbits who served. These were friends from his youth, who had helped him to take power into his own hands.

And so it became necessary to have even those rabbits, whom he trusted, shadowed as well. The complexity of his present situation didn't allow him to say: These and these rabbits can be freed from surveillance, because he trusted them, and others had to be shadowed. That would resemble a Law, which should relate to each one without partiality.

"I don't even exclude myself," the King said to the Chief of the Guards. "If you discover that I have joined a conspiracy against my own legitimate power, then punish me, as you do with the others."

"Just try and get involved in such a conspiracy," the Chief of the Guards replied threateningly, and this calmed the King.

After all, if you introduce a law about secret surveillance, it should apply to everyone equally, the King thought. After all, if you tried to divide all the rabbits in his service who were under surveillance into those who had to be shadowed and those who didn't, this could evoke crude and mistaken notions in the guards' minds about the possibility that there were rabbits who were trusted in everything and rabbits who weren't trusted at all. In fact, things were a good bit more complicated, and the truth was dangerously subject to modulation.

If those who were being followed found out there were some who were not, they could get rather offended and even incite a conspiracy against the King deep in the underground.

But so could the rabbits who weren't under surveillance. Precisely because everyone around them was being tailed, and they weren't, the law of temptation would make them aspire to take advantage of the possibilities that arose because of this situation.

But in the meantime, having established surveillance over his childhood friends, whom he trusted, the King was conscience-stricken. The friends of his youth, who noticed that they were being watched, realized that the King didn't trust them, and so they began to be more reserved in his presence, that is, they became more secretive from the King's point of view.

But, nevertheless, whenever he thought about the friends of his youth, he suffered some remorse, and because of that it was unpleasant for him. Time passed, however, and the King gradually forgot why he had experienced any unpleasantness when he recalled the friends of his youth.

All he felt was that they were instilling a certain unpleasant feeling in him, and he decided that this feeling was evoked by their suspicious reserve.

Without even noticing it, he tried to justify his hostility toward his childhood friends by taking into account the reports of those who were watching over them. Every time he listened to these reports about their lives, he displayed such a lively and greedy interest in everything about them which could seem suspicious that the surveillance rabbits couldn't help but feel this. And having noted the King's vital interest in everything suspicious, they — at first unconsciously and then consciously — began to stress everything in their reports that would evoke some lively interest in the King.

And as odd as it may be, precisely the fact that his childhood friends were absolutely clean helped the guards. In such instances, precisely the clean rabbits had to face the most dangerous slander.

A being whose profession it is to bring to light the possibilities of inimical thoughts or deeds in another being sooner or later cannot help but try to discover such thoughts and deeds. For if nothing is discovered over a long period, it becomes only too clear that his profession is not needed.

But why should a cleaner rabbit have to suffer more in such cases?

By not giving any real details of enmity, he forces the rabbit checking up on him to ascribe to him, sooner or later, a certain baseness. And not just a little villainy. But why "not just a little?" That's how the rabbits' psychology is structured. Ascribing to a rabbit, who must be informed on, the concealment of an extra carrot from the royal storehouse? That would be really silly! In order to justify somewhat the baseness of a report, the informing rabbit makes the imagined villainy sufficiently significant, and that helps him to preserve a feeling of his own dignity. It's one thing when a rabbit imputes to another rabbit a part in a conspiracy against the King, and another matter entirely when he ascribes to him this extra carrot, which wasn't handed over at the royal storehouse.

The rabbits' psychology is so amusing in its makeup that it's simpler for the informer to demonstrate that an innocent rabbit has formed a conspiracy against the King than it is to show that an innocent rabbit is pilfering a royal carrot from the storehouse.

In the latter instance, the boss, to whom this is reported, could quite reasonably ask:

"Exactly who saw that he was stealing a carrot?"

And then the informer must produce some convincing evidence.

But if the informer has reported to his chief about a conspiracy against the King, of which this rabbit or that is a member, then his boss can't ask him:

"And where exactly is the proof that this conspiracy exists?"

And why can't he ask that? Simply because that's the way the rabbits' psychology is fixed. When some rabbit or other is accused of treason against the state, demanding proof that this treason exists is considered to be terribly tactless by the rabbits. Such a delicate, such an intimate question about one's loyalty to the King (or the lack of it), and suddenly to have it followed by some coarse, visible, material evidence, that would be like demanding a public demonstration of the rabbits' erogenous zones on the rabbits' ideological hide. From the rabbits' point of view, that would be unattractive and even scandalous.

And would it really be surprising, if an informer were to hear his boss demand evidence of the rabbit's complicity in a plot, if the informing rabbit shouted, in an outburst of patriotic rage:

"Aha! You don't believe that a conspiracy exists?! You must belong to it yourself!"

In the rabbits' kingdom, the most frightening thing of all was to be under fire because of patriotic rage. According to the rabbits' customs, patriotic rage had to be always and everywhere encouraged. Every rabbit in the kingdom, at the moment when he displays his patriotic rage, instantaneously occupies a rank higher than the rabbits against whom his patriotic rage is directed.

There was only one weapon against patriotic rage — to become superpatriotic and rage even more than one's opponent. But it was usually very difficult to do this, because a certain momentum was needed, and it was almost impossible to gain enough momentum to be even more patriotic than the rabbit who had confronted you with his patriotic rage.

Due to these reasons the informers' bosses decided not to demand evidence when the conversation turned to this or that rabbit's treason against the King.

And, having committed an injustice in regard to his former friends, the King was prepared to expect, in the depths of his soul, that they would try to avenge themselves for his injustice. And when testimony about their treason began to surface, he accepted it with greedy satisfaction. Soon none of his old friends, with the exception of the Poet, remained close to him. But was he really close?

At first the Poet reminded the King about his great plans, and the King unfailingly replied that he remembered everything well, but unfortunately now he had to attend to all the matters connected with the throne, which made him run like a squirrel in a cage. And besides, he had ordered that several more tubs of ink be prepared for the time when universal education would come to the rabbits.

At first the Poet's conscience bothered him, and he decided that the least he could do was not to write anything that directly praised the King. But something kept him from abandoning the life at court and the luxury, to which he, and most importantly his family, had grown accustomed.

"After all, the King is doing something for the future," his wife would say. "You know there are those new tubs of ink in the royal storehouse."

"We'll just have to wait, we'll see," the Poet comforted himself, and he did what he could, including not writing verses that praised the King.

When the King began to destroy his friends, the Poet experienced not only the pangs of conscience, but also the torment of fear.

He thought that the King was exaggerating the danger, but apparently where there's smoke there's fire, and after all, they weren't arresting the Poet. They weren't hanging him up by his ears, as they were doing with the other rabbits.

Once the King invited him to a nighttime orgy, where they drank well-fermented floral nectar and enjoyed the company of the court ballerinas. And so, lest he offend the King, the Poet had to join in the festivities, along with everyone else. However, the King himself unexpectedly freed him from his hardly persistent pangs of remorse.

"Oh, sometime we'll get something from our Poet," the King joked at the height of the orgy. Without even realizing it, he thereby implanted a great dream in the Poet's heart. The Poet decided that from now on his life would be devoted to unmasking the King with his wrathful poem, "The Storm of Disillusionment." And he felt better immediately.

Since then he hadn't missed one of the King's sinful diversions, justifying his attendance by avowing that he had to see, with his own eyes, so that the revelation could be profound and comprehensive.

"What is this to me? For me this is all just material," the Poet used to say, swallowing the floral nectar or embracing the court ballerinas. The Poet very quickly became accustomed to his material, which he was preparing to expose later with his wrathful, satirical pen. Sometimes it seemed strange to him that he again and again tried to experience those base, voluptuous pleasures which he had already experienced. It still seemed to him that he hadn't quite sensed all the fine details of the King's moral degradation.

And yet he was sincerely preparing to write his poem, "The Storm of Disillusionment." He was thinking about beginning it as soon as he had distanced himself from court life. And he was getting ready to move away from that, as soon as he learned all the details about the King's degradation. He thought it would be amoral to begin the poem while he was still enjoying all the privileges of court life.

Thus he decided not to waste any time and to begin working out the poetic rhythms of his future literary expose.

He very much liked working on rhythms without the words. On the one hand, his wrathful outbursts weren't wasted, and on the other, their sense remained inaccessible to the court spies. He would create some rhythm, write it down on a magnolia leaf and hide it in a drawer. He also wrote down the sense of the rhythm's future intentions in an abbreviated form, so that it wouldn't be forgotten.

Sometimes he read these rhythms to the King, and the King always praised the freshness and the aggressive explosiveness of each new rhythm.

Once he read a rhythm to him that expressed his anger about the King's slowness in the matter of the rabbits' universal education.

Approving of the rhythm, the King said:

"That's fine for you, you speak directly with God, but I have to deal with rabbits. I wish you would fill in that rhythm with a fiery denunciation of those rabbits who delay paying their taxes from their garden raids."

Having heard this request, which directly contradicted the sense of his rhythm, the Poet lost his composure and agreed to comply with the King's request. It seemed to him that the King suspected him of something, and in this way, he decided, he could dispel his suspicions. He went home and wrote the verses he had been ordered to compose.

But in the meantime, this iniquitous use of his rhythm about justified rage evoked a new flood of even more furious rhythms in the Poet's soul, and having written this down, he was at last calm. As usual, he put a title over the transcription of his rhythm — in order to conceal its true meaning: "Repeated Rage Apropos of . . . "

"The King will pay dearly for humiliating me," he said to himself, imagining how he would lash the King when he filled the rhythms of repeated rage with words.

Now, each time the King with his unpardonable requests humiliated his divine — well, if not exactly divine, then at least righteous — rhythms, a new rhythm of protest began to grow in the Poet's soul. And he wrote down this protest, so that in the future he could unmask the King with even more caustic lines in his poem, "The Storm of Disillusionment." And so now, whenever he read his new rhythms to the King, he awaited each new humiliating assignment with Samoyedic pleasure.

By the way, once when he was complying with one of these humiliating assignments, he chewed off the upper end of his goose quill pen and accidentally sucked up some of the fermented elderberry juice ink, and he experienced a new wave of inspiration. Later, as we have already said, his discovery became the property of the whole nation of rabbits.

Finally, he made the decision to leave the court, in order to begin his poem, but right then his wife blocked the way. She said that it was fine for him to leave the court right now, he had already lived out his best years, but how would it be for his adolescent son to abandon the court, when a great career was just now opening up for him.

"Just get our son set up well, then we'll leave," she said to him, "and for now you can still collect rhythms."

And he got his son fixed up with the Royal Guards, and because of this he had had to hold a humiliating conversation with the Chief of the Guards, whom he didn't like because of his cruelty, and who in turn despised the Poet because of his verses.

But even after that, he found he couldn't leave the court. His stubborn wife began to fall into hysterics, because the splendid poetic isolation he dreamed about wasn't a place well suited for his daughters, who were preparing to marry rabbits from the court circle.

"Let's get our daughters set up first," she sobbed, "And you can still collect rhythms for now."

"Well, I've really got enough of them," he tried to convince his wife.

But not one poet has ever been able to make his wife

listen to reason, and he was forced to wait until his daughters were married. And during all this time he continued to participate in the King's various diversions, although he still hadn't taken part in any of his perfidious frauds.

And precisely at this time, the King had thought up a cunning way (or so it seemed to him) of removing the suspect rabbits. The fact is that capital punishment didn't exist in the rabbits' vegetarian kingdom, and removing those suspicious rabbits with the boas' help was too troublesome. And so here's what he thought up:

He announced an annual competition for the position of Wise Old Rabbit. As you know, the Wise Old Rabbit had obtained his post because a carrot-shaped acorn had hit him on the head while he was standing in the shade of the carrot oak tree, and it had caused a concussion. And by having this concussion, the rabbit proved irrefutably that there was something to shake up in his head, and thus they named him to the post.

Since that time, the King compelled the suspicious rabbits (and the King considered suspicious precisely those rabbits who advocated any improvement in governing the kingdom) to take part in this competition for the position of Wise Old Rabbit.

"We'll see," he said. "If it turns out that you are the Wise Old Rabbit now, then we'll give your proposals serious consideration."

The rabbits who were suspected of pretensions to the position of Wise Old Rabbit were put under the carrot oak, after which the tree was shaken at the top, in order that the falling carrot acorns could cause concussions among the competitors.

Usually several rabbits perished after this because of direct hits by the acorns. Then the remaining rabbits continued the competition of the victors, and finally, when one last rabbit was left, he either renounced his pretensions to the position of Wise Old Rabbit, or if he didn't renounce his claim, then the court doctor declared that he had not had a concussion for the simple reason that there was nothing to shake loose in his head.

The Poet not only didn't condone this mockery of naive, vain rabbits, he sobbed when he watched this spectacle. The court rabbits tried to spare his sensitive heart and tried to lead him away from the carrot oak; but he continued to sob, he was stubborn and didn't leave.

"No," he said, "I have to drain this cup to the dregs."

And then, wiping his eyes, he managed to steal a glance at the sky, apparently expecting to see a consoling stormy petrel in flight.

It's interesting to note that during the annual competition, several rabbits who weren't suspected of anything at all ran into the area where the acorns were falling, right when the oak was being shaken the strongest. They hoped that wisdom would suddenly be discovered in them, and that they would be worthy of the position of Wise Old Rabbit.

Observing this picture of wisdom being sorrowfully elicited, the Poet not only created a rhythm, which expressed his stormy protest, but he also risked his position by filling in the beginning part with words. He then read it to a very small circle of trusted friends.

> Let a storm burst forth upon the world,
> And strike the carrot oak!

After he read these lines, he silently put the magnolia leaf, on which he'd written them, into his desk, and his astounded friends exchanged glances and shook their heads, thus showing that they'd grasped the meaning behind the reckless audacity of the coded part of the poem.

"You know, the carrot oak grows right next to the royal palace," one of them finally uttered.

"That's the whole point," another added.

The reckless audacity, however, subsided at this point.

The Poet thought, and not without reason, that while he was still a member of the court and was still taking advantage of the excesses in food and the passionate overindulgences of the nighttime orgies, he had no right to oppose the King.

But although his daughters did get married, a new obstacle then arose. It turned out that a person who worked in the Royal Guards, that is, his son, a rabbit with access to the Guards' secrets, did not have the right to have distantly placed relatives, and even less any relatives who had voluntarily left the court circle.

And so he had to help his son leave the Guards and get him transferred to a job with the treasury. Another year went into getting this accomplished.

But then it was revealed that in one more year, the rabbits were going to mark twenty years of the Poet's irreproachable service to the King, and according to the laws of the kingdom, he was to receive the title of First Royal Poet. This title didn't give him any privileges during his lifetime because he already had everything, but after his death it gave him the right to be buried in the Royal Pantheon, among the most esteemed rabbits of the kingdom.

To withdraw from the court just before receiving this title would be an act of unprecedented rudeness, and yet leaving it afterwards would be considered brutish ingratitude, and so he remained there for several more years.

He was already old now, but still life would have been too unbearable if he had given up on his intentions. Once, while sifting through his dried magnolia leaves, which were covered with the future rhythms of the future poem, "The Storm of Disillusionment," he began to laugh quietly.

"What are you going on about?" his wife asked; she had just returned from the royal storehouse where they received their produce.

"Oh, just that . . . " he said, carefully putting away the pile of yellowed magnolia leaves, so that his leaves wouldn't get scattered, "that my supply of rhythms reminds me of the King's reserves of ink.''

''Ah, there are all kinds of coincidences,'' his wife replied, spreading the fresh produce from the royal storehouse on the table.

Yes, the Poet remembered now — his family wasn't the most serious obstacle. His wife would of course bitch a little that they'd been deprived of the court produce allotment, but she wouldn't really stop him. The obstacle was in the Poet himself.

He was old enough to be thinking about his own death. He knew that if he died, and he were still part of the court, he'd be buried in the highest tier at the Royal Pantheon. Of course this right would formally remain his, even if he were to leave the court, but who knows how the King would take his departure.

What a tragic contradiction, he thought occasionally, no one except me could help my corpse to get a fitting burial.

''If I could,'' he used to say to his wife, ''bury myself with honors, then leave the court and calmly write my poem.''

''Well, don't get upset,'' his wife replied, ''they'll bury you with honors . . . ''

''If I remain here at the court, of course they'll bury me,'' the Poet responded, ''but we're planning to abandon the court . . . It really would be ideal for me to bury myself with honors, then write my poem, 'The Storm of Disillusionment,' and then die peacefully . . . ''

''You want too much,'' his wife replied, ''any other rabbit would be satisfied with discovering such a wonderful, invigorating drink for the rabbits . . . You've already done so much for the nation, let others try to do things now . . . ''

''Well, let's hope that I did something,'' the Poet responded, considering how to fix things up for his future corpse in the best possible way, and at the same time trying to elicit a new poetic rhythm from his sorrowful musings.

His situation was so hopeless that sometimes he gave himself over to the gloomiest fantasies. He thought about trying to pretend to be dead, letting himself be buried in the Pantheon, and then, secretly abandoning his luxurious crypt, fleeing to the jungle and calmly writing his poem there.

But he had enough common sense to understand how risky the whole project was. And even if he succeeded, the thought about his vault's inferiority tormented him. Of course others would think that he was lying in his wonderful vault. But he'd know it wasn't so, he'd know that if he weren't reposing in his own crypt, that would basically mean the crypt didn't belong to him.

And so, without having found a way out of this tragic contradiction, the Poet fell ill, and one fine day he died. Just before his death, the King and his aides had visited him, and having wished him good health, the King hinted that in the event of his death, he would treat his corpse in the best possible way.

And the King lived up to his promise.

Banners with the depiction of the Cauliflower hung over the Poet's body. The King himself and all the Admittees stood in the honor guard, and young rabbits read the Chief Poet's verses.

He was buried in the Pantheon, and the heap of magnolia leaves with the rhythms of the future poem were transferred to the royal archives. The kingdom's Chief Scholar deciphered all the rhythms to his future poem and found for each rhythm a corresponding verse, which had been included in the royal collection of poetry.

Thus, for the rhythm titled "Rage Apropos of Slowness . . . " he found a poem ridiculing those malicious rabbits who failed to pay their produce tax. and for the rhythm called "Repeated Rage Apropos . . . " he found a poem which ridiculed all of the former and perhaps even more who hadn't paid this tax.

And so all the rhythms of our tragic failure of a poet were deciphered in this primitive way, which offered later generations the opportunity to reaffirm that the Chief Poet of the rabbits was a rather talentless rhymester.

It's true that the more educated connoisseurs of poetry avowed that the Poet had had an early period when he had composed divine verse, and that only later, under the King's influence, did he begin to write nonsense.

But other, even more refined experts (perhaps they were even more refined detractors?) affirmed that even in his earlier poems an evident lack of certainty in respect to the truth was noticeable. That is, they had in mind uncertainty about the ultimate and independent value of truth, which was, in their opinion, the only sign of strength and life-giving fortitude in any creation. And just this lack of certainty in the Poet's soul, in their opinion, later led to the lamentable downfall of his talent.

Unfortunately, those debatable, or questionable, products of our Poet's earliest creative period have not come into our possession, and so we do not have our own opinion in regard to them. We simply put forth the opinions of later connoisseurs in order to acquaint readers, who might be interested in this question, with the very fact that such an opinion exists.

For all of this touches on a somewhat later story about the rabbits' kingdom. Our topic is essentially their kingdom's flowering in expectation of the Cauliflower.

5

Let's return now to the events taking place when we interrupted our story. The following day, a merry little ditty was heard in the jungle:

A pondering someone
Sits upon a little hill.
Sa-va, Sa-va, Savannah
And Fro-go-ro-go Ford!
But a storm is fast approaching!

Of course, that was Sharpie's voice. He had already sung this not terribly difficult verse several times, but no one had responded to it. All the better, Sharpie thought joyfully, I got the song so mixed up that the devil himself would break his head trying to figure it out. And what's more, I myself risked removing the main word in the third line: view . . . Just try to guess: who was pondering, what was he pondering, and who benefited from the fact that he was pondering?

He sang the verse one more time, and not hearing the familiar, loathsome rustling in either the grass or the bushes, he calmed down completely and went on even quicker. If I go very quickly, then I'll get through the Neutral Path more quickly, and not one boa will be able to understand what I'm singing about, Sharpie thought, amazed at his own mental acuity. Now he was skipping along, singing his ditty on the run, and only stopping occasionally to catch his breath and reassure himself once again of the pleasant lack of result from his singing.

This time Sharpie stopped under the shade of a wild pear tree, which grew right at the edge of the Neutral Path. Here he decided to catch his breath and at the same time feast on the pears which had fallen from the tree, that is, if the wild boars hadn't gobbled them up already.

And just then two marmosets, a momma-marmoset and a daughter-marmoset, looped their tails around a branch high up in the pear tree and swayed there a little. Having heard Sharpie's song approaching, the momma-marmoset stopped swinging and listened with alarm to the singing. The daughter-marmoset also listened to it.

"The king of the rabbits is betraying someone again," the momma-marmoset said. "Just listen to that herald's repulsive voice."

"What's that — Fro-go-ro-go Ford?" the daughter marmoset asked.

"That's Frogs' Ford," the momma-marmoset said, starting to swing by her tail once again. "There's only one consolation (push! sweeping with her arms to swing harder), that no matter how many of these heralds I've seen (another push! and stretching out her arms to swing even harder), they don't outlive their victims by much."

"That means betraying is the same as killing," the daughter-marmoset guessed, "only not with your hands?"

"Yes," the momma-marmoset agreed, having reached the necessary height with her swinging. "Betraying always means killing someone, but using someone else's hands to do it, as the natives say . . . And now follow me. See how loose I keep my body? As soon as you swing up to the highest point, you let go with your tail and fall, and don't think about anything. But as soon as you've flown to the branch you want, you flip your tail around it very lightly, and the rest of you will keep on flying for a little while. Your tail will lash itself tight, and you'll be hanging solidly from the branch."

"But for some reason, my tail doesn't hold me and I fall," the daughter-marmoset replied.

"Because you're so afraid that you snatch at all kinds of liana vines on your way down," the momma-marmoset responded. "You don't have enough speed to make your tail lash tight. Remember — the main thing when you're dropping vertically is having enough speed for your tail to lash tight. Falling is nothing, it's the lashing speed that counts. Look, I'll show you again."

"One," she said, increasing her swing and at the same time relaxing her body, to show that she wasn't concerned at all about what could happen to it, "two, three . . ."

The momma-marmoset hurtled down, adopting an expression of tranquility, the kind of facial expression the native women have when they knit clothes made of animal hair. Just then her tail curved ever so slightly around the branch she had chosen, and in a moment it had lashed itself tightly to the branch, because it had been jerked by the force of her body's weight.

"You understand?" the momma-marmoset asked from below, looking up at her daughter.

"I understand," the daughter replied, not very certainly, looking downward to where her mother was swaying and even farther down, where Sharpie was walking in the shade of the tree, gathering the pears which had fallen from the branch the momma-marmoset had fastened onto.

Having eaten some of the pears, Sharpie paused to admire the marmosets as they gamboled. Suddenly he had a sad thought, that they had it really good, hopping from branch to branch, not having to worry about any songs or any royal missions.

"Well, who's stopping you?" he heard a voice inside him say suddenly.

"What do you mean, who?" he replied aloud, because it had happened so unexpectedly. "If nature made me a Sharpie, than I have to strive to do my best at that."

He listened intently, expecting that the voice inside him would respond, but for some reason it didn't say anything more to him.

"Looks like there's no response to that," Sharpie said sternly to the voice and moved along. He got as far as the end of the Neutral Path and turned back, thinking about what kind of mischievousness was going on inside him. He still really wasn't quite himself. And the main thing was that the voice had suddenly started up and then just as unexpectedly fallen silent. If you've decided to pick a fight with me, then do it, Sharpie thought, but then what came of it? It was suddenly there and then suddenly disappeared, but it's wrecked my mood. Well, so what, just to spite you, I'll sing it again.

> A pondering someone
> Sits upon a little hill.
> Sa-va, Sa-va, Savannah
> And Fro-go-ro-go Ford!
> But a storm is fast approaching!

He sang it out and listened to the jungle. He didn't hear a single alarming sound in the area immediately around him. Well then, I'll just sing it one more time, he thought, directing his comment to that voice, and that's all. I'll be free!

But suddenly he heard that despicable hissing in a bunch of ferns; the invisible body of a boa constrictor was moving toward the river, slinking through the ferns, making their tips move slightly. It really doesn't matter which of the boas is slithering along, Sharpie thought in fear, trying to console himself. No, no, I don't believe it's creeping over there!

And in order to prove to himself that he didn't believe it, he began to sing the song very loudly, without stopping.

And his thoughts raced feverishly through his mind right then. Why didn't I join the regular rabbits! he thought. But I couldn't go back to the regular rabbits! he corrected himself right away. Oh, if only I'd eaten the Queen's gift, then I could have joined the regular folks. Oh, if only! he thought, continuing to sing, and at the same time going back to safety along the Neutral Path.

And after all, what if that boa was just slithering all by itself toward the river, maybe it already turned off in some other direction long ago . . . Sharpie thought, trying to rid himself of the anguish which was making everything so unpleasant for him. There's the pear tree, he said to himself, if the marmosets are there, I can find out from them if the boa has been there. Maybe he's already moved off in another direction.

Meanwhile, the momma-marmoset and daughter-marmoset were still working on vertical leaps. In the interim, the daughter had managed to fall out of the tree, because her tail hadn't caught the branch. She was listening to her mother, and scratching her smarting side, while the mother explained the finer points of jumping.

"But I didn't just clutch at the branch right away, and still it didn't work for me," she was saying in her defense.

"It was precisely because you weren't catching onto it," the momma-marmoset was explaining to her, swinging by her tail and looking up at her daughter from below. "You were even more frightened, and because you were afraid, your tail stiffened. Your tail should be completely relaxed at the moment when it's supposed to be catching hold. Then you get enough of it wrapped around the branch to ensure complete safety . . .We'll try it again . . ." The daughter-marmoset wrapped her tail around a branch, and she had just started swinging her arms to get started when she suddenly noticed a boa slithering by on the Neutral Path beneath her.

"A boa!" she screamed. "I'm afraid."

"It's going toward the river," her mother was a bit more specific.

"But did the herald cause all this?" the daughter exclaimed.

"Who else but him?" the momma-marmoset sighed. "C'mon, he's slithered far enough away now."

"Wait, momma," the daughter said. "I'm shaking all over . . . And when I think that Ponderer is sitting there on his hill, and a boa is slithering toward him, a boa sent by one of his fellow rabbits, it makes me sick . . ."

"Calm down and try it one more time," the mother said, "the main thing now is to keep your tail loose . . ."

The daughter-marmoset just couldn't calm down, for

some reason. Just then they heard the cheerful sound of that treacherous song. The Royal Herald was returning, coming back along the Neutral Path.

"What's he singing about?" the daughter-marmoset was surprised. "I mean, doesn't he know that the boa has already been by?"

"Of course he knows," the momma-marmoset replied, "he's doing it on purpose, so that no one will think that the song and the betrayal are connected in any way. He could say: 'I was just singing it by myself, and the boa stumbled upon Ponderer all by itself' . . ."

"That's really clever!" the daughter shouted. "Aren't the natives descended from the rabbits?"

"I don't know," the mother said, continuing to swing by her tail and listening to what was happening on the Neutral Path, "they say they're descended from the apes, from us . . ."

Meanwhile, Sharpie had approached the pear tree and he again saw the same marmosets on the same branch of the wild pear tree. These were the first creatures he had seen after his act of perfidy, and it was pleasant for him to see them. It suddenly seemed to him that nothing in the world had changed, everything was the same as before. Here's a wild pear tree, it was growing there before, it's growing now, the marmosets on it were working on their vertical leaps before, they're still doing it now. And everything, ev-er-y-thi-ng is the same as before . . . He suddenly wanted to talk with someone, in the worst possible way, even with these marmosets.

"Hey, up there in the tree," he called from down on the ground. "Shake your branch and knock some pears loose. I want to treat myself to some pears . . ."

Silence. All he could hear was the rhythmic squeaking of the branch the momma-marmoset was swinging from. And again Sharpie felt ill at ease and flat.

"You don't want to part with any, is that it?" he shouted up at them.

Again silence. Had the boa really slithered over toward the river, where Ponderer was sitting?

"Listen," he shouted again to the marmosets, "has anyone walked by, in the direction of the river?"

Painful silence. But a monkey, or a marmoset, can't be silent for long.

"You meant to say — has anyone slithered by?" the momma-marmoset finally responded venomously.

She knows, he thought in horror, and at the same time he was infuriated by this overly impudent marmoset.

"I wanted to say precisely what I said," he replied haughtily and then fell silent.

"Oh, look how insolent he is," the daughter whispered.

"I'm gonna jump down and spit in his face," the mother whispered back decisively, "and you watch how I fasten my tail on the branch . . ."

"Spit in his face, momma, spit in his face," the daughter whispered gleefully and began to fidget with excitement on the branch.

The momma-marmoset swung on the branch and then flew down. Her tail caught on the very lowest branch, right over Sharpie's head. The branch she had looped her tail around snapped like a whip, and a hail of pears fell to the ground. Sharpie, who was terribly frightened by this unexpected occurrence, at first didn't immediately understand what was going on, despite his mental acuity. He didn't know yet that a creature who commits an act of treachery is ready to take any surprise as the beginning of retribution.

"Oh," Sharpie finally caught his breath, "is that you, marmoset?"

"No, it's an angel sent from heaven to punish you," the marmoset replied caustically, swinging on the branch.

"What do you mean, a punishing angel?" Sharpie replied coldly. He had already managed to regain his composure and take on an expression more befitting a Royal Herald.

"Oh," she said, "just that you can stop singing your

song, because someone has already slithered somewhere a long time ago . . .''

"Why are you talking about a boa constrictor?'' Sharpie screamed, losing his self-control. "I won't permit it! I'm a Royal Herald! I'll complain! I will, I will!''

"Slow down a little. I didn't say anything about a boa constrictor,'' the marmoset said, as she kept swinging on the branch.

"No, you said it!'' Sharpie screamed, "that's an outrage! That's mockery of a Royal Herald! You're doing your training over the Neutral Path. I won't let things go on like this.''

And in fact it wasn't permitted to train over the Neutral Path, and in general it's better not to get mixed up with this rabbit, the marmoset thought. Having put off spitting at him, she silently climbed back up, while Sharpie went on gesticulating with his ears and muttering something.

"Well, what about it, did you spit on him?'' the daughter asked, when her mother had climbed to the top branch and sat down next to her.

"I'll say!'' she replied.

"And so what'd he do?'' the daughter asked.

"What'd he do? He wiped it off and went along.''

"Momma,'' the daughter-marmoset said, "what if I run over and warn Ponderer. . .''

"It's not really worth getting involved,'' the mother answered, and then added, "well, you know, it's probably too late . . .''

"But what if I succeed!'' the daughter exclaimed. "I can leap horizontally very quickly.''

"No, and that's final!'' the mother said in an even sterner voice. "You're still little, too little to get mixed up in things like this.''

"Mommy, mommy! I beg you! I'll run! I'll fly! I'll make it!'' the daughter implored her mother.

"No!'' her mother replied even more sternly and rigidly.

"There's a lot you still don't understand . . . I also feel sorry for Ponderer . . . His teachings have some interest for us too . . . but he's already gone too far . . . Too far . . ."

"But I feel sorry for him," the daughter broke into tears, finally grasping that her mother wasn't going to let her go anywhere. "He's just sitting there and thinking, but he's already been betrayed."

"What can we do?" the mother sighed. She set her daughter on her knees and began to stroke her head. "The natives say that science is like a divinity, which demands sacrifices . . . If the rabbits stop grazing in the natives' gardens, maybe the question of us having to leave the natives' corn alone will arise. Nope, Ponderer has gone too far."

"But after all, momma, you said yourself that the natives are descended from us," the daughter reminded her, now calming down gradually, rubbing her head against her mother's chin. That's how she usually reminded her to look for fleas on her head.

"First of all, I'm not the one who says that they do," the mother said, and she began to click her nails, digging around on her daughter's head. "And second, when it comes to corn, they forget about how they're related to us and hunt us with dogs and set their traps, loathsome traps, like the jaws of a crocodile . . . Well, what do you say, want to try the vertical leap again?"

"Not today," the daughter replied sadly, "I'm too worked up . . ."

"Then let's go home," the momma-marmoset said. "We'll tell the others everything we've seen and heard . . . I wonder how it'll all turn out . . ."

"Let's go," the daughter agreed sadly, and then they hopped over to a magnolia and disappeared in the lustrous foliage of a magnolia grove.

Meanwhile, Sharpie had walked nearly the entire length of the Neutral Path, and came out at a smallish meadow, which was situated not far from the first rabbit settlement. He had been thinking all this way about what had happened, and now he'd almost calmed down and forgotten about the marmosets.

First of all, he thought, that boa could have been moving toward the river all on its own. Second, maybe Ponderer's right, maybe the boa couldn't swallow him. And third, look at those clouds coming up from the south. A storm's going to start any minute, and Ponderer's not going to sit out on an open hillock in a storm. And the more opportunities he found for Ponderer to save himself, the more cheerful he became.

And suddenly, right there in that meadow, by the first rabbit settlements, he met Ponderer's wife.

"What are you doing here?" he asked her, after changing the initial greetings.

"Well, I'm putting in a little clover for the winter," she sighed as she replied. "My husband just thinks all the time . . ."

"You have some assistance from the King," Sharpie was surprised.

"Two carrots, with six mouths to feed?" she said, raising her head. "No, I'm grateful to the King, but still I have to keep running around . . ."

"It looks like there's going to be a storm," Sharpie said ponderously, and looked at the sky. In fact, some very black, very promising clouds had scudded in from the south.

"Well, I live right by here," she said, looking quickly at the sky.

"Listen, your husband, if he's caught out in a storm, does he come back home?" Sharpie asked suddenly.

Right then Ponderer's wife decided that Sharpie was hinting about something. At one time in their youth, both of these rabbits had been in love with her, but because she had been young, she'd chosen Ponderer, a choice she very much regretted now.

"What are you talking about?" she said and waved her paw. "He sits there from morning to night and thinks. No, in the daytime you can't get him to come home with a stick . . ."

"Well, actually," Sharpie said, "he's on an open hill. What if he got wet for a whole day?"

"Oh, I know better," she replied, looking Sharpie in the eye, "so come in, I'll serve you whatever there is . . ."

"No thanks," Sharpie said, having finally caught her hint, and having decided that this would really be too much. "I have to report to the King now . . ."

"Sure," she sighed, "you're such a big shot now . . . Don't have anything to do with us anymore . . ."

"Ah," Sharpie waved his paw, "It's nothing special . . . Well, I am an Admittee to the Table, I can eat all I want, drink all I want . . . But that's not true happiness . . ."

"All of you talk like that," Ponderer's wife sighed again, "and I have a sore mouth because of this clover . . . My husband, the fool, he could have been where you are, but he didn't want to."

"Well, okay, good-bye," Sharpie said and moved along, feeling that his mood was getting progressively worse.

"Good-bye," she replied, and begun cutting clover with her incisors again. "Well, if you decide to, drop in . . . We aren't rich . . . Whatever we have . . ."

Sharpie nodded vaguely and went through the meadow, cutting across it so that he could come out nearer to the Royal Meadow.

6

Ponderer was sitting on his green hillock near the river. The savannah stretched out to his left, and on his right there was a good view of the vast Frogs' Ford. Ponderer observed life around him with a sad, and at the same time, penetrating gaze. Actually, it would be better to say that Ponderer observed life around him with a penetrating gaze, which was sad precisely because of his penetration.

Right then a mosquito wasn't being very careful, it flew too low over Frogs' Ford, and a frog snapped it up. Then a frog wasn't looking out, and a heron stabbed it with the point of its beak. But then a heron, which was enviously eyeing the other heron swallowing the frog, was caught off guard and a crocodile nudged it into its terrible maw. And then the natives caught the napping crocodile, after which they cut it into mouth-watering (or so it seemed to them) morsels, loaded it onto the boat and set off for the other shore. But they hadn't managed to reach their village before one of them, who had bent down too low over the water, managed to be dragged out of the boat by another crocodile.

"And they call that living," Ponderer said, nodding to Yearner, who was sitting next to him.

"Teacher," Yearner replied, "it still seems to me that if you had just promised the rabbits that we could keep on stealing, we would have won the case. You were so close to victory. I mean really, isn't it possible to lie just once, for the sake of our wonderful goal?"

"No," Ponderer answered. "I've thought about that many times. Precisely because a vital life is always moving and changing, we need the orientation of something as hard as a diamond, and that is truth. It might not be the complete truth, but it can't be consciously distorted even for the sake of the grandest goal. Otherwise everything falls apart . . . A sailor can't get his bearings from falling stars."

"But after all, the victory was so near, Teacher," Yearner reminded him of that great day when the rabbits had almost gotten rid of their King.

"Nevertheless, it's not possible," Ponderer repeated.

"After all, if we overcome the Great Injustice in regard to the rabbits, the possibility of avoiding a tiny injustice in regard to other creature's gardens will still arise. Moreover, other tiny injustices in the rabbits' lives will come to light, including some new ones. For example, the rabbits might be proud and announce that they had rid the jungle of the terror caused by the boa constrictors, that they're now the leading creatures . . . There's a lot that could happen . . .

"And remember, as soon as we free ourselves from the Great Injustice, it will be instantly forgotten by the ordinary rabbits, it will disappear. And then any of these new, petty, unpleasant tendencies will seize those spiritual forces, which had previously been taken up by the rabbits' fatal fear of the boas. That is what life is like, that is the law of anxiety renewal, the law of life's self-preservation."

"But really, things right now are worse," Yearner objected, feeling that Ponderer was going too far. "The rabbits have remained loyal to the King."

"For now — yes. The rabbits' consciousness has been corrupted by the boas' tremendous baseness. But they have accommodated their base little deeds to this tremendous baseness, even including the baseness of stealing from the natives' gardens. It's our difficult task to shatter this consciousness."

"But where is the certainty, Teacher?" Yearner asked. "And what if everything stays the same?"

"There is something higher than certainty — that is hope," Ponderer replied. "Yesterday I was sitting here alone, and today you've come here, even though it's dangerous and not really to your advantage."

"Well, okay," Yearner again objected. "We didn't have to lie. But couldn't you have kept quiet about those damned gardens the natives have? We could have gotten the King out of the way, and then we would have had the most opportune possibilities for shattering that consciousness."

"No, no, and no," Ponderer repeated. "I've thought

a lot about that. All the liberators' causes have perished because of that. Each one of them has been carried away by his own noble task and has willy-nilly considered it the final victory over the world's evil. But as I've already said, when what is evil now disappears, what is evil tomorrow will appear instantaneously. All the unwise liberators failed to understand this, and therefore, once they achieved victory, they became senile from not understanding life around them.''

"But what about the wise liberators?'' Yearner asked.

"The wise liberators,'' Ponderer smiled ironically, "didn't live to see their victory . . . But why did the unwise ones, who were triumphant, become senile?'' Ponderer continued. "Because they didn't understand the law of the renewal of anxiety, they perceived the forgetfulness of those who were liberated from evil (from which the liberators had helped to free them) as monstrous ingratitude. Therefore, they artificially compelled the liberated ones, who were inclined to forget about their own liberation, to celebrate holidays of liberation. In the final analysis, the liberators and those they had liberated shared a profound, secret, and mutual hatred.

"The liberators thought they had made their fellow tribesmen happy, but that the stupid creatures couldn't realize it, so they tried day and night to pound it into their consciousness.

"Those who had been liberated knew that the liberation hadn't made them happy, and so they were angry with their liberators for promising to make them happy, which they not only failed to do, but they also compelled them to admit what they didn't feel — precisely this happiness at being liberated.

"Having lost their ideal, they begin to idealize the victory. The victory goes from being a means of attaining the truth to the truth itself. Remember this aphorism: victory is the truth of scoundrels. Whenever they talk a lot about victory, they've either forgotten the truth or they're hiding from it. Just recall how the boas love to talk about their daily victories over the rabbits, and remember how our hypocritical King announces the impending victory of the rabbits with each casual decrease in the number of rabbits swallowed by the boas, and calls every rise in the number of rabbits lost a temporary success for the boas."

"That's when we should have deposed him, right then," Yearner kept trying to hammer his point home. "If you'd just kept silent, when everything was smelling of cabbage."

"No, no and no," Ponderer kept on repeating, just as stubbornly. "I've thought a lot about that. All the reformers' causes have perished because of that."

"You already said that, Teacher," Yearner interrupted him, "your thoughts reach me better when you point out something by using examples from our life . . ."

"Fine," Ponderer said, and added, after he had thought a little while: "Here's an example for you. Imagine that one generalized boa is chasing the whole nation of rabbits. The rabbits are tired, they're on their last legs, and finally they're approaching a river, which will save them. The river saves them because the rabbits are able to ford it, but the generalized boa, just imagine, is afraid of water.

"If the rabbits reach the water, they will most definitely be saved. But many of them are barely dragging themselves along. And it's about one hundred hops to the river. So, does their leader have the right, in order to cheer up those losing strength, to shout: 'Rabbits!' Give it one more effort! It's only twenty hops to the river!'"

"I'd say he has that right," Yearner said, trying to imagine this whole scene. "Then, when they have been saved, he could explain the facts."

"No," Ponderer said, "that's how all the reformers have made their mistakes. After all, the task of saving the rabbits never ends. Having crossed the river, the rabbits only get a breather. Our generalized boa will find some log that has fallen across the river, either upstream or downstream, and it will continue its chase. After all, the boa is a generalized one, and there will always be connoisseurs of rabbit meat.''

''That means, I think, that there is a right to lie only in the most extreme cases.''

''No,'' Ponderer said, ''there is no such right. No matter how grateful the rabbits may have been to their leader for encouraging them with his lie, it will always remain in their consciousness that he was able to lie. Thus, the next time, they will take his signal of danger as a conscious exaggeration. But the leader too, although he lied in the name of truth, has already betrayed truth, he has dishonored it. And the more he has dishonored it, the less he is able to respect it . . . It will annoy him . . .''

''Lord, how complicated this all is!'' Yearner exclaimed. ''What can we do?''

''Shatter the rabbits' certainty about the boas being able to hypnotize them. In accordance with his nature, a rabbit might stumble, not really wanting to, out of weakness, and even engage in some revelry in a garden, but his ideal should remain as firm and pure as a diamond. I've already said that a sailor can't get his bearings from falling stars.

''And the main point isn't the number of mistakes or errors, but something else. If a rabbit comes to after debauching himself in a garden and realizes how he has fallen, his future is not lost. The defeat begins when he starts to justify his fall as a part of his nature, or the law of the jungle. That's when the betrayal of the ideal begins, that's when the lie, from which there is no exit, starts.''

''Teacher!'' Yearner unexpectedly shouted, ''a boa is slithering over here. That's the first time I've seen a boa hunting in an open space.''

''Well, so what?'' Ponderer said. ''After all, you know that their hypnosis is our fear.''

"Y-y-yes, in general," Yearner stammered, "but what if all of a sudden . . ."

"Then step aside, and you'll see that everything I've told you is true."

"I feel ashamed, Teacher, but my fear is stronger than I am."

"I'm not condemning you . . . You haven't thought long enough yet. When, after long and tormented contemplation, you discover a grain of the truth, you will defend it fearlessly . . ."

"But still, Teacher . . . You know, that was a one-eyed invalid. We could, perhaps, hop away before it's too late . . ."

"I'm not going to give the King that satisfaction," Ponderer replied, watching the boa creep up on his green hill, where he had spent so many days contemplating the fate of his fellow rabbits.

Meanwhile, the boa had slithered into sight on the hill. It was the same young (no longer little) boa which had once heard Squinter tell all about his misadventures.

He had been the first to hear the herald's song, and according to the customs established among the boas, he had the "right to the first swallow." From time to time the King essentially handed over various rabbits, by means of various heralds, and the boas had long since grown accustomed to this.

The right to the first swallow was considered a gift of fate, a sure thing. At first the young boa had been quite overjoyed that he had won this right, but now he wasn't as content.

To begin with, on his way here, he had met a mole and asked it about the best way to get to the little green hill facing Frogs' Ford. And what do you know? The mole sent him off in the wrong direction; he had wasted several hours in the jungle, and he'd had a lot of trouble finding that damned green hill.

Finally having understood that the mole had fooled him, he was shaken by the senselessness of this deception. Why? Why did it deceive me, the boa thought, and he couldn't understand it at all. First of all, boas generally don't even touch moles. And second, the mole generally didn't know where he was creeping and why. Well now, if he'd been fooled by some wild goat or turkey, then everything would have been understandable. Rabbits aren't the only things boas eat. But why would a mole fool him? To whose advantage is this? After all, it's clear that the mole gains nothing by this deception. Then why? Why?! Why?!

Now, having reached the green hill, he was unpleasantly struck by the sight of the open space, where there wasn't a single tree, not a single bush to hide behind, to lie in wait for the prey. What a barren locality, he thought, God keep me from living here.

Having slithered to the top of the green hill, he suddenly discovered that instead of one rabbit, there were two waiting for him. He knew that rabbits can multiply very quickly, but he never knew that it happened with such incredible speed. And really, which one of them is Ponderer, and who gave birth to whom?

Creeping slowly, he looked them both over from a distance, trying in any case to impress on both rabbits that he was getting ready to swallow it, and only it. Now, having approached the rabbits, he tried to breathe more calmly and not reveal his tiredness. It was considered customary for boas to appear — no they had to appear — fresh, full of joyful energy, in good spirits, before they swallowed their prey.

"Listen to me attentively," Ponderer said, "I'm going to conduct an experiment with that boa; you stand at the side and observe. What is the distance at which their hypnosis is effective today, according to the forecasting bureau?"

"A distance of three hops, Teacher!" Yearner exclaimed, without taking his eyes off the boa that was creeping nearer.

"Draw a line two hops away from me," Ponderer said calmly.

"But isn't that dangerous, Teacher?!" Yearner tried to object.

"Don't argue, we don't have enough time," Ponderer hurried him up.

The boa had already crept to the crest of the green hill and was about ten hops away from them. Yearner didn't waste any more time trying to plead with Ponderer. He hopped twice away from the Teacher and toward the boa; these weren't among his most successful hops, though he very much wanted to risk his life for his Teacher.

Nevertheless, he drew a line, as the Teacher had said, and immediately hopped away from the boa, about ten hops away, and each of these hops was amazingly successful, although he was restraining himself with all his might. Now he was sitting at a fairly safe distance and following what was happening, his heart palpitating with excitement.

The boa slithered closer. He still couldn't decide which of these two rabbits he had the right to swallow. And what if one had given birth to the other, then couldn't he apply his right to swallow both of them, pleading tardiness? Or premature birth in the process of swallowing? Or was it worth it?

The strange actions of the rabbit which had first jumped in his direction and drawn some sort of cabalistic sign, and then had hopped away somewhere inspired strong doubts in the boa. Something's not right here, he thought, trying to be as circumspect as possible.

Now he felt a contradiction in the movement of his huge body. The part of his body that was closest to the head noticeably slowed its movements, while the tail portion coiled nervously, as if it were annoyed by the slowness of its forward part. And the tail beat on the grass impatiently, raising tiny spurts of dust.

Having slowed his forward movement to the limit, the

young boa carefully drew his head near the line, tested it with his tongue, and looked it over carefully, trying to grasp its insidious purpose.

"You see," Ponderer said, "even a boa which is torn from its normal circumstances is immediately at a loss."

"Yes!" Yearner shouted in extreme agitation, "I see, but the tail section is putting a lot of pressure on him!"

"That's how it should be," Ponderer explained calmly, "his belly gives the orders, and the boa's head only serves to help in the swallowing process . . ."

And then the boa stopped, in complete and total indecision. He even narrowed his eyes a little at the second rabbit, thinking he might want to take off after it. This unexpected little line, and the rabbit's calm voice (this was the main thing), confused him too much.

But right at that moment Ponderer finally fell silent, his ears drooped, and his eyes began to look pleasantly tired. The boa again took heart and without taking his eyes off the rabbit, he moved his head over the line. The rabbit was rather thin, and a thought flashed through his mind that the King of the rabbits betrayed precisely these skinny rabbits, so that he could eat the fat ones himself. He knew, of course, that rabbits don't eat other rabbits, but right then he'd forgotten that.

"Teacher, Teacher!" Yearner shouted, "it looks like you're falling asleep! Wake up!"

"Don't be upset, everything is going normally," Ponderer replied calmly, trying not to frighten the boa with his voice.

"But why take such a risk, Teacher?" Yearner again shouted.

"My inexperienced boa isn't doing its job with any spirit," Ponderer replied, "and so I'm helping it . . ."

The boa, fixing its loathsome gaze on Ponderer, continued to slither slowly across the line.

"What makes the boa's gaze so frightening," Ponderer

continued his observations, "is the complete lack of thought
. . . Basically, what is a boa constrictor? A stomach that
slithers."

"Teacher, it's very close now!" Yearner screamed in
horror. "Hop to the side!"

"It's okay, I'll be all right," Ponderer replied and con-
tinued observing the boa.

The boa continued to slither toward him, concentrat-
ing all his efforts on the sacred ritual of hypnosis, that is,
trying not to take his eyes off the rabbit. But this time some-
thing strange, something unusual happened. The young
boa's nerves were too strained.

The rabbit that was about to be swallowed was behav-
ing offensively. And the main thing was a flow of informa-
tion coming from it — and where was it going? Toward a
rabbit that wasn't even in swallowing range. The Great Py-
thon never allowed such lapses.

The young boa was now so sorry that he'd set out on
this adventure (even though it had been such a sure thing!),
he hated that herald so much! But there was nothing he
could do, it was too late to retreat now . . .

"Listen to me," Ponderer continued in a calm voice.
"I'm completely within the sphere of the false hypnosis.
I don't feel anything except its breathing, and it's true that
it has rather bad breath . . . I am in complete control of my
senses and appendages. My speech, from the point of view
of science, should serve as evidence of complete sanity.
Remember this in case the King declares that everything
I say is the result of hypnotic delirium. Now I am about to
undertake a series of actions, in an order I will predict in
advance."

"Hurry up, Teacher, hurry up!" Yearner shouted, so
excited that he was hopping up and down.

The boa was already about one hop away and was
listening to Ponderer's words with alarm. Several times he
had been about to reply to these insults, but the strict cus-

toms of his fellow boas forbade him from talking or entering into a discussion with a rabbit about to be swallowed.

"And so, I'll move my right ear," Ponderer said, "Then my left. Then both at once . . . And then I'll sniff three times, at regular intervals . . ."

And suddenly the boa was bathed in cold sweat and noticed in horror that the rabbit's right ear raised up and moved. And then, breaking the sacred ritual, he shifted his gaze to the left ear, which also raised up thoughtfully, and moved sort of reproachfully, although he was using all of his hypnotic powers to order (even to beg with humility) that rabbit not to move.

After this, to the boa's complete fright, both ears moved at the same time, and in accordance with what it had predicted, the rabbit began to sniff. And right then the boa's nerves gave out.

"I can't work like this!" he shouted. "Why are you sniffing in my face?" Why are you wiggling your ears and talking?"

"Everything's correct! Victory! Victory!" Yearner exclaimed, dancing and clapping his paws. "You did everything exactly as you had said, only you sniffed four times!"

"The last time I sneezed," Ponderer corrected him. It was clear from his voice that he was satisfied with the experiment he had just conducted. "The boa really smells . . . By the way, I'm not excluding the possibility that this is the basis for the legend about hypnosis. It's possible that one of our ancestors couldn't stand the boa's breath and fainted. The air in the jungle was cleaner then, because there were a lot fewer natives. And this may have served as the cause for panicky rumors . . ."

"Victory! Victory!" Yearner began to shout, dancing in place. "The triumph of reason!"

"You don't have to misuse the word 'victory'," Ponderer corrected him, "even if it is the triumph of reason, I'd like to throw out that word entirely . . . I'd like to replace

it with the word 'overcoming.' I hear the stamping of fools'
feet in the word 'victory' . . . But I'll stop talking now, it
seems that my boa has completely lost its energy . . .''

And with these words Ponderer fell silent, lowered his
ears and began to close his eyes. The boa tried again to pick
up where he had left off, but he was overcome by tremen-
dous tiredness; he got weak and lay down.

"I have to catch my breath," he said, trying to conceal
his embarrassment. It was a rather shameful confession, but
he'd already started talking, so he had to explain the cir-
cumstances too.

"Rest," Ponderer agreed, "only watch out you don't
fall asleep, and please breath in another direction . . .''

"I've been unlucky from the very start," the boa said,
trying at least partly to justify his listlessness. "And if you're
so smart, then give me an answer to the question of why
a mole would want to fool me, what was its aim, what ad-
vantage could it gain by doing that?"

He told about how the mole had deceived him when
he was setting out to capture Ponderer and swallow him.
By the way, he judiciously omitted the name of the rabbit
which had sent him here.

"If it'd been a goat kid or a wild turkey," he repeated
his argument, which seemed irrefutable to him, "I would
have understood why they would have wanted to fool me.
But why would a mole deceive me, what advantage would
it have?"

"Because a mole is a wise animal," Ponderer said, "I've
always known that."

"That's no answer," the boa objected, and then, hav-
ing thought a little, he added, "It didn't know where I was
going and why, did it?"

"Yearner," Ponderer turned to his pupil, "pay atten-
tion to this particular, though curious case. The mole is wise.
But if wisdom is powerless to do good, it does the only thing
it can — it lengthens the path of evil."

"But what if I were hurrying to help a comrade?" the boa objected again.

"Hah!" Ponderer grinned, "No one's ever heard of a boa helping its comrade."

"Why not?" the boa said, trying to recall some appropriate instances from the life of the boa constrictors. "Who helped Squinter when a rabbit stood up crosswise in his stomach?"

"First of all, that's past history," Ponderer smiled ironically again, which seemed especially unpleasant to the boa, "and second, we know how they helped him . . ."

"Well, so what?" the boa said, even more wounded by Ponderer's correct surmise, "in any case, boas don't betray each other, and rabbits do."

"Where did you get that idea?" Ponderer inquired

"Well, what do you think? Why did I turn up here?" the boa asked maliciously. He felt that Ponderer wasn't familiar with the richness and variety of forms used to betray others.

"I don't know," Ponderer replied, "there are a lot of places where a boa could wander."

"Then you should know," the boa replied, sensing that the superiority of knowledge is also a considerable pleasure, "that your King, through his herald, announced that you were here. And the herald this time was the rabbit called Sharpie."

The young boa had betrayed the herald without any hesitation. He was peeved at him for all this trouble. And so that Ponderer wouldn't have any doubt, he even ran through the herald's song.

"Do you want me to decipher it, so you won't have to bother yourself?" he asked Ponderer.

"It's clear the way it is," Ponderer responded, profoundly saddened by this treachery. "I didn't expect this, not even from our King. Did you hear, Yearner?"

"I'm stunned," Yearner exclaimed, "perhaps it's a provocation?"

"No," Ponderer said sadly, "I recognize the undistinguished style of our court Poet . . . Well then, I'll go along with the King's perfidious intentions to the bitter end, so that later you can expose him . . ."

"What do you mean by that, Teacher?" Yearner shouted in horror.

"I'll have to sacrifice my life," Ponderer said wistfully and simply.

"Don't do that, Teacher!" Yearner exclaimed. "It will be difficult for me without you . . . And then the King will announce that he was right, that your death was the result of incorrect scientific conclusions."

"But what about you?" Ponderer replied, "you've seen everything. My death will open the eyes of our rabbits to their King. And now you know everything about hypnosis, and you can repeat everything . . ."

"But all the same, Teacher," Yearner begged, "I implore you not to do this!"

"No," Ponderer said, "I didn't know that our King had sunk so low that he was capable of handing over rabbits to the boas . . . Now anything could be expected of him. He could announce that I had conducted my experiment on a sick, anemic boa. But no, this one is completely healthy, a normal boa, and now it's going to do what it's supposed to."

"No, I'm not going to swallow you!" the boa screamed unexpectedly and slithered backward a little. After everything that had happened here, he felt terribly uncertain about hypnosis and was now afraid to disgrace himself. He even turned away slightly from Ponderer, just as capricious creatures turn away from foods they find objectionable.

"Good for you, boa!" Yearner shouted, overjoyed, "for once you're doing something good in your life."

"Call it what you want," the boa hissed scornfully and again stole a look at Ponderer, trying to feel how skinny and tasteless his body would be.

"So, that means you won't be swallowing me?" Ponderer asked sternly.

"You're right, I won't!" the boa shouted, annoyed. "First the herald promised a surefire thing, then that mole deceived me, and here you fiddle with your ears and talk and sneeze in my face!"

"I won't allow you to spoil my experiment, I want you to know that!" Ponderer said and looked so severely at the boa that it seemed even more like a coward.

"Let's part on a friendly basis," the boa offered peaceably. "I'll say that I didn't find you, that the mole diverted me from my goal on top of that. And you were being fruitful here, multiplying . . . How do I even know which one of you is Ponderer? Maybe you want to sacrifice yourself to save the real Ponderer."

"We're both Ponderers now," Yearner said, partly to confuse the boa for the last time, and partly from pride.

"That's exactly right," the boa agreed, "I was given the right to swallow one Ponderer, and there are two of you here. I don't even understand how you could give birth to each other. Which one of you is the female?"

"You see how poorly he knows us?" Ponderer said. "The myth about omniscient boas is the result of rabbits' fears."

"Judging by everything," the boa felt offended again because the rabbit had insulted all the boas, "you also didn't know your own rabbits very well . . ."

"That's the bitter truth," Ponderer agreed, "but I'm going to force you to swallow me!"

"Never!" the boa exclaimed, "a rabbit cannot command a boa to swallow itself!"

"You still don't know how much stronger your stomach is than your rationality," Ponderer said and began to freeze.

The young boa turned disdainfully away from him, looked several times at him lasciviously, and having convinced himself that the rabbit wasn't moving, he began to come to life again and stretch out toward him.

"Of course," he muttered, looking at Ponderer with the uncertain, thus particularly impudent gaze of a dishonored hypnotizer, "after a long journey, it's no sin to have a bite to eat . . ."

"Teacher!" Yearner shouted, "your death will be like a retreat. You'll be abandoning our cause . . ."

"Quiet," Ponderer stopped him calmly, "or else you'll frighten it again . . . I loved my fellow rabbits and did everything in my power. But now I'm tired, Yearner. Treachery has broken me. I knew many of the rabbits' weaknesses, knew many of the King's cunning traits, but I never thought that a vegetarian would be capable of spilling his own rabbits' blood. I've given so much time to studying our enemies that I let my own enemies slip from sight. Now I fear for myself, I fear that my soul will sink into tremendous indifference, something that usually happens with rabbits on the gloomiest day in the very middle of the rainy season. And other rabbits shouldn't see me that way . . . You will carry on the cause of reason. And it will be easier for you in many ways, easier than for me, but also harder. It will be easier because I'm handing over all my experience in studying boas, but you, dear Yearner, will have it harder because your love for rabbits near to you will have to accustom itself to the possibilities of treachery. My love didn't know that and so it was easier for me . . . I hand over to you our cause and therefore I claim the right to be tired . . ."

The boa was slithering toward Ponderer all this time, trying not to think that Ponderer was a rather skinny rabbit, but rather that he was the smartest rabbit, and that by swallowing him he would be depriving the rabbit nation of their smartest rabbit, and at the same time would be compelling him to serve the boas' cause.

"Teacher!" Yearner shouted for the last time and began sobbing, because the boa's jaws had just closed around Ponderer.

"I'll show that bastard, the King!" Yearner sobbed bitterly, "I'll show that big shot Sharpie! Those bastards, they've detroyed a great rabbit!"

The boa slithered away unnoticed, moving his jaws and listening to Yearner's sobbing, and at the same time tasting the rabbit he'd swallowed. He was almost ashamed that he had swallowed such a remarkable rabbit, but he was equally ashamed of the long, humiliating ceremony involved in swallowing this rabbit.

It had all turned out rather clumsily, he thought, though now all of his mind is in me . . . That's right. But what if there really is no hypnosis? Or maybe mine stopped working? No, I'm simply too tired . . . In any case, one thing's right — all of his mind is in me . . . After I digest him, when his body becomes my body, his mind will have no place to go, and it will become my mind . . .

That's how the young boa thought, slithering off into the jungle, trying to chase away all the alarming thoughts about his hypnotic powers. But his thoughts suddenly turned from alarming uncertainty to the most glorious hopes.

In the end, he thought, what does hypnosis mean to me? Having the double mind of a boa and a rabbit, I can become the first among my fellow boas. The Great Python, for example, doesn't catch rabbits at all, they feed him prepared ones . . . And it's not known yet which of us will be smarter. And in general, the thought flashed through his mind, why should a python rule over the boa constrictors? It's true that he's related to us by blood, but still he's an alien.

"A boa should rule over the boas!" he suddenly hissed aloud, struck by the profoundity and precision of his thinking. It's already working, he thought, and what'll it be like when the rabbit has been completely digested?

Then he finally calmed down and, finding a warm little spot in a thicket of ferns, he coiled up and began to doze, trying to become smarter by absorbing Ponderer.

7

That very same day, the news about Sharpie's treachery spread throughout the jungle, helped in part by the monkey who reported about it, one could say, at the highest levels of the jungle, and in part, of course, by Yearner himself.

The rabbits were in a state of furious agitation. Some of them said that it just couldn't be, although all kinds of things can happen in life. They felt sorry for Ponderer with all their hearts. At the same time, they experienced a combined feeling of shame and secret relief. They felt that the burden of doubt, which Ponderer had been trying to instill in them, had finally been lifted.

An uncertain life under the conditions of a security they wanted and an honesty they didn't seemed much more difficult to them than their present life, which was full of foreboding dangers but also of penetrations, excited by a whiff of sweetness, into the natives' gardens. And thus they felt an even strong sense of relief the more heatedly they expressed their sorrow about Ponderer, their outrage about this act of treachery.

And although they had never wanted to follow his wise advice, now when he was gone, they sincerely felt like orphans. It turned out that the rabbits needed one of their own who could urge them to the path of truth, even if they weren't prepared to walk along that path.

Towards evening, almost the entire population of rabbits gathered at the Royal Meadow in front of the palace. The rabbits demanded a special meeting. It began to look like a revolt, and before declaring the meeting open, the King ordered the guards to clear the emergency exits of the royal palace. He always had the emergency exits put in order whenever there were alarming meetings such as these.

"The better an emergency exit is," the King used to say to those rabbits Admitted to the Table, "the fewer chances there are that it will be needed . . ."

This time the situation was quite disturbing. As always, the flag with the picture of the Cauliflower had been raised above the royal dias before the meeting began. Despite the fact that the colors used to depict the Cauliflower were now mixed together in the most mysterious and significant way, the rabbits paid almost no attention to the flag. Once in a while one of them would glance at the new pattern of the Cauliflower with an expression of empty curiosity, then wave its paw and dip back into the nearest whirlpool of the seething crowd.

Finally, order was somehow established. The King stood up. Slightly below him stood Sharpie, who was frightened and looked around in all directions, his eyes bulging.

"The excitement is preventing me from speaking," the King began in doleful voice, "truly frightful words are passing through the crowd. Rabbits have accused me, the father of all the rabbits, almost of treachery."

"Not almost, but exactly — treachery!" Yearner shouted out from the crowd.

"So be it," the King let slip unexpectedly. "I'm above personal vilification, but let us explain what the facts are . . ."

"Go ahead!" they shouted from the crowd.

"Down with the King!" others shouted. "What do we need to have explained?"

"And so," the King went on, "why did the herald turn up on the Neutral Path? Yes, yes, I personally sent him there. But why? Unfortunately, my friends, according to the evidence which has been coming to our chancellery recently, the number of rabbits who have disappeared without a trace into the jaws of boa constrictors has increased sharply. It inevitably follows that the boas have recently been more insolent. It's possible that rumors about Ponderer's new theories had reached them, and they decided to demonstrate the power of their fatal hypnosis.

"What was there left for us to do? To show the enemy that we were becoming submissive, that we had fallen into despair? No and no! As always, we decided to respond to the deaths of our fellow rabbits with a crushing boldness of spirit! They swallow us, but we sing! We sing, therefore, we're alive! We're alive, therefore, they won't swallow us!!"

(Right then stupendous applause broke out among those Admitted to the Table and those Aspiring to be Admitted. Later, in all the reports of the meeting, because of some odd mistake, this applause was termed "stupendous applause, which turned into a general ovation." It's possible that it was planned that way, because the King stopped at this point, perhaps expecting that the applause would turn into an ovation. But the applause, which was not a true ovation, stopped, and the King continued to speak.)

" . . . And so, our herald was sent with his song to the Neutral Path, where he was to sing, as stipulated in our royal journal by the way, the text of the melody 'Variations on the Theme of the Stormy Petrel,' set to the rhythm of a march."

"The words, the words!" rabbits shouted furiously from the crowd. Some of them used fresh bamboo shoots as whistles. At a meeting, this was considered disturbing the peace, and if the rabbit was caught whistling by a royal guard, he was forced to pay a fine. But the fact is that the guard usually didn't find the whistler because the rabbit who had whistled ate his whistle right away if a guard started coming toward him.

"The text was actually composed by our own court Poet," the King said; he glanced around, finding him, as if by chance, among those Admitted to the Table. And he nodded to him. "Let's have him recite his own divine rhythm . . ."

The Poet had been crying for a long time over Ponderer's fate, deep in his heart damning the King's cunning, because he had forced him to write that poem. But now he had to think about his own fate, and even though he continued to whimper about Ponderer's demise, he did figure out quickly, with the assistance of a hint from the King, how to extricate himself from this mess.

He stepped forward, continuing to sob, and announced:

"The text, actually, is rather conventional . . . It was supposed to sound . . ."

"We don't know the fine points," the King interrupted him, "you just recite to the rabbits here what you wrote."

"By all means," the Poet said, jerking his shoulder in a sort of scornful embarrassment; and he went on:

"Actually, I wanted to preface the text with some explanations. I was able to find an original phonetic structure, which could smother the triumphant psyche of the boa constrictors with its oppressive cheeriness, that is, I meant to say . . ."

"The text! The text! The text!" the rabbits shouted and whistled with their bamboo whistles. "You don't have to explain anything . . ."

"Actually, I wanted to preface . . ." the Poet said, but then, jerking his shoulder again, he read:

> Pom-pom, pim-pim, pom-pim-pam!
> La-la, li-li, la-la!
> Pim-pam, pam-pam, pim-pim-pam!
> But a storm is fast approaching!

"That's actually what he was supposed to have sung, of course to the melody of 'Variations on the Theme of the Stormy Petrel.'"

The Poet sat down at his place, looking up at the sky, searching for a stormy petrel that might happen by.

"There are variations, and there are variations," the

King repeated the last words threateningly and turned to Sharpie to ask him:

"And what did you sing?"

"Exactly those same words," Sharpie squeaked, stunned by the treachery of the King and the Poet. And like any traitor who is betrayed, he was stunned by the vulgarity of the way he had been betrayed. He couldn't understand that only the person being betrayed can sense the vulgarity of any betrayal. The one responsible for the treachery can't feel it, with the same force at any rate. Thus the betrayed traitor, recalling his own feelings at the time when he was carrying out his own treacherous act, and comparing them with his own feelings about when he himself is being betrayed, thinks with complete sincerity: still, I didn't sink that low.

The stunned Sharpie hadn't managed to squeak out his self-justification before the voice of a marmoset rang out from above.

"That's not true!" she shouted, hanging from a coconut palm, "I heard everything, and so did my daughter!"

"The marmoset heard everything!" the rabbits shouted, "let the marmoset tell us everything!"

"My brothers, dear rabbits," the marmoset shouted, looking at the upturned rabbits' faces, "friends in the natives' gardens! My daughter and I were sitting in a pear tree near the Neutral Path. I was teaching her the vertical leap . . . And I was telling her, when you fall vertically, you have to loop your tail firmly . . . "

"You don't need to tell us about that! To hell with your damned vertical leaps!" the rabbits began to interrupt her. "Tell us about what happened!"

"Okay," the marmoset nodded, somewhat offended, "if you're such egotists, then I'll leave that part out . . . So, I'm teaching my daughter . . . and suddenly I hear the herald moving along the path below, and he's singing this song:

> A pondering someone
> Sits upon a little hill.
> Sa-va, Sa-va, Savannah!
> And Fro-go-ro-go Ford!
> But a storm is fast approaching!

A fearsome sound of indignation, whistling, and stamping was heard in the crowd.

"Traitor! Traitor!" some of the shouts could be heard distinctly. "That 'pondering someone,' that's our Ponderer!"

"I understood right away that he was betraying Ponderer," the marmoset screamed, "and then I spit in his face!"

"Good for you, marmoset!" the rabbits shouted. "Death to the traitor!"

"How could he distort my text like that!" the Poet exclaimed; as a matter of fact, he was truly indignant about the way his text had been distorted. He's twice a traitor, the Poet thought: once, for distorting my text, and twice, for betraying Ponderer. And because he felt betrayed, the Poet forgot about his own measure of guilt in Ponderer's betrayal: what kind of traitor could he be, if he let himself be betrayed!

The King looked angrily at Sharpie. The rabbits gradually calmed down, waiting to hear what he would say.

"That means," the King turned to him ominously, "you actually sang:

> Sa-va, Sa-va, Savannah
> And Fro-go-ro-go Ford?"

"Yes, Sharpie confessed, barely audibly.

"And was that the way I taught you to sing it?"

"No," Sharpie was frightened and he was about to say, "You asked me . . . "

"Silence!" the King shouted, "answer to the people; did you introduce your own variation or not?"

"I did," Sharpie affirmed, nodding his head, totally crushed. After all, he had left out a word in the third line that the King had insisted upon.

"He introduced his own variation," the King repeated with pitiful sarcasm. "Where did you change the text? Change the royal text, did you? When did you do it? Just now, when the boas are currently oppressing the rabbits and the experiments on raising Cauliflower have never before been so close to completion?"

"The King is not to blame," the rabbits shouted with redoubled energy, overjoyed at the prospect of not having to riot now. "Long live the King! The scoundrel introduced his own variation!"

"But why did you do it?" the King shouted, gesturing accusingly with his paw. "Don't say it to me, answer to the whole nation!"

"Brothers, have mercy," Sharpie cried, "I repent, I repent! But why did it turn out this way? All the time I'd been thinking about what Ponderer had said. I very, very much liked everything he said about hypnosis. I believed him with all my heart. And so I decided: the quicker he's able to show our King and all of us that he's right, the better it will be for everyone. Brothers, I didn't know it would turn out this way . . . "

"Who asked you!" the indignant crowd shouted. "Traitor, scoundrel!"

"Let me through," the heart-rending wail of Ponderer's widow rang out, "I'll scratch the eyes out of that Judas!"

"Forgive me, brothers!" Sharpie howled.

"There's no forgiveness for a traitor," the rabbits replied, "you're gonna end up inside a boa, brother!"

Finally, Yearner stood up and gave the best speech of his life. He spoke about his Teacher's last minutes. He told everything about what he'd seen and heard. Many rabbits sighed deeply when they heard his story, and the females sobbed. Even the Queen cried. She dabbed her eyes with cabbage leaves, one right after the other, and when they were damp, she threw them into the crowd of rabbits, which, despite the grieving, evoked an embarrassed rush among the crowd each time.

Yearner passionately called on the rabbits to develop their doubts about the omnipotence of hypnosis, and at the same time to continue Ponderer's cause.

At the end of his marvellous speech, he attacked the King. He said that even if the herald had come up with his own variation, the King, who had selected the herald and traitor, was not worthy to be King. Therefore, he said, they finally had to make use of that rabbit law, which for some reason had never been invoked, and they were to determine, with the aid of a vote, if the rabbits were ready to choose another King. At the very end of his speech, Yearner promised before everyone that on the next holiday, he would run back and forth along any boa. He would dedicate this dash to the memory of his Teacher.

When he finished speaking, a huge majority of the rabbits applauded him furiously. It was obvious from their faces that they were ready not only to select another King, they were already visualizing the future King rather clearly.

However, both those who applauded and those who withheld their applause waited with great curiosity to find out what the King would do. And at the bottoms of their hearts, they wished the King would do something to outsmart them, although they couldn't give a good account of why they would want that! They just wanted him to, and that's all!

The King had abandoned his royal dias, it even seemed that he had waved his paw in disgust, although he hadn't actually done that, it had just seemed he had. It seemed to mean something like: I'll give up the throne now, without even waiting for your vote. And so he stood there, sorrowful and silent, waiting for the applause to end.

"Rabbits," he finally began to speak, quietly, in a voice that was devoid of any hint of personal interest, "I would like to propose that while I am King a moment of silence be devoted to the memory of our great scholar, our beloved brother Ponderer, who perished heroically in the jaws of a boa constrictor while conducting his experiments, which we supported materially, even though we didn't agree with them theoretically . . . His widow won't let us lie . . . "

"That's the whole truth, oh Provider!" the widow was about to wail from the crowd, but the King cut off her lament with a wave of his hand, lest she destroy the solemnity of the sorrow.

The rabbits were amazed that now, when others had been talking about deposing him and selecting another King, he was troubling himself about Ponderer, and not worrying about himself.

Everyone stood in sorrowful silence. Meanwhile one minute passed, and then another, a third, a fourth . . . The King stood there, as if lost in reverie, and no one dared to break the silence. It was somehow not very flattering, not noble to say that the minute of silence had been over for a long time. This was one of the King's great devices for secretly making a crowd annoyed with one of its idols.

The King, seeming to come to, made a motion that loosened his hold on his subjects, encouraged them to sigh deeply, and then to proceed to their inevitable duties in life, even if those duties meant ending his reign.

"And now," the King said with noble restraint, "you may choose another King. But according to our laws, I have the right to express my last wish before the election. Am I right, rabbits?"

"You're right, you're right!" the rabbits shouted, touched by his magnaminity.

"No matter who you choose to replace me," the King went on, "it's necessary to have good health and discipline in the kingdom. Now, under my guidance, you will have some productive gymnastics, and then immediately after that we'll move on to the voting."

"Go ahead," the rabbits shouted, "otherwise, our blood will cool."

With a wave of his arm, the King ordered the court orchestra to play, and with a voice that overpowered the orchestra, he began to direct the state gymnastics.

"Rabbits, stand!" the King ordered, and the rabbits hopped up.

"Rabbits, sit!" the King commanded, and with an energetic flourish he seemed to glue the rabbits to the ground.

"Stand! Sit! Stand! Sit!" the King said ten times in a row, gradually increasing the tension and speed of the commands, along with the music.

"Now, rabbits, let's vote!" the King shouted, though the music had stopped. He continued with the same rhythm, and the rabbits jumped up to vote, although it wasn't obligatory to stand to vote.

"Rabbits, who's for me?" the King shouted, and they hadn't had a chance to come to their senses before they found themselves with upraised paws. Everyone except Yearner had raised his or her paw, and a bunny who happened to be near Yearner raised two paws, suddenly afraid that he might be suspected of something.

The royal accountant was about to begin counting the outstretched paws, but the King looked over his people, and with an extremely democratic gesture displayed public disdain for any kind of petty counting. He waved his arm as if to say that the algebra of harmony needn't be demeaned.

"Rabbits, who's against me?" the King asked in a more tender voice.

And only Yearner raised his paw. The King nodded good-naturedly at him, as if approving of the very fact that he had fulfilled his civic duty.

"Rabbits, who abstained?" the King asked, in a tone that showed he knew, of course, there were none, but the law was the law and he had to obey it.

Having given ample opportunity to those nonexistent abstainers to make themselves known, and not having seen any, the King said:

"And so, what do we see? Everyone is for, only two are against."

"But who's the second one?" the rabbits were surprised and looked at each other, standing on their tiptoes in order to get a better view of the crowd.

"I'm the other one," the King said loudly, and raised his hand, so that everyone could understand what he was talking about. After that, he looked at Yearner, and added: "Unfortunately the people who support me don't support us in our votes . . . "

"Look at that!" the rabbits laughed, feeling rather tender about their King, because he was dependent on them, on their votes, and they, simple rabbits that they were, they hadn't let their great King down.

The King was in a happy frame of mind again. He was thinking that these outwardly simple, practical exercises he'd come up with some time ago were actually a great device for keeping submissive reflexes alive, for refreshing them from time to time.

"I will therefore continue to carry out my difficult duties," the King said, enjoying himself and winking to the crowd. "What do you say about Yearner's offer?"

"Let's have a show, a demonstration!" the rabbits shouted gleefully.

"Did you mean there and back," the King asked Yearner, winking at the people.

"There and back!" Yearner replied seriously.

"One way on the inside, and back on the outside?" the King asked, to the laughter of the other rabbits.

"No," Yearner replied, "there and back on the outside."

"A boa of your own choice, or any boa?"

"Any boa."

"Rabbits," the King addressed the people. "Will we

choose a slightly longer boa, for the sake of folks being able to see the spectacle?''

"A longer one!" the rabbits shouted. "It'll be more interesting that way!"

"Okay," the King said, "we'll have to make an arrangement with the Great Python . . . But keep in mind, Yearner, that a boa will agree to this humiliation only if it gets the right to the first swallow."

"Of course," Yearner said calmly, "I'll dedicate that dash to the memory of my unforgettable Teacher."

"Of course," the King responded, "as soon as we strike a bargain with the Great Python, we'll set up a show for our whole nation."

"Long live the King! Long live the Teacher! Long live shows!" the rabbits shouted, finally satisfied with everything.

"By the way, what should we do with the one who betrayed Ponderer?" the King asked and motioned Sharpie to come over to him; Sharpie had used the opportunity of the King and the other rabbits being diverted to slink quietly into the crowd, though he didn't dare conceal himself in it. Sharpie stepped out of the crowd and stood before the rabbits, his head bowed.

"Death to the traitor!" the rabbits shouted, having caught sight of Sharpie and recalling everything again.

"We cannot put him to death," the King said thoughtfully, "we're vegetarians."

"What about feeding him to the boa that Yearner will run alongside?" one of the rabbits asked.

"Very clever," the King agreed, "but we can't because we're vegetarians. And there wouldn't be any scientific benefit. What risk is there in being hypnotized if the boa knows ahead of time that it's already been promised another rabbit?"

"Like my Teacher," Yearner said proudly, "I can risk only myself."

"I propose," the King said, "to banish the traitor forever to the desert . . . Let him chew on saxaul plants for the rest of his life . . . "

"Let him chew on saxauls!" the triumphant rabbits repeated.

"Take him away now and escort him there," the King commanded, and two guards dragged Sharpie away as he looked at the King and Queen and all those Admittees with the beautiful eyes of a drowning kitten.

"You'll learn how to fashion your own variations," the King muttered, trying to justify himself in front of those beautiful eyes.

"Deceiver," the Queen said, sorry that she hadn't managed to get her fill of those eyes, which were now disappearing for no good reason. "He himself said: 'Never.' But he ate my gift."

"He's young. He'll be good at chewing on saxaul plants," the Wise Old Rabbit said. "Just imagine if I'd been sent away then."

The old egotist, who was looking at the suffering rabbit and recalling that he could suffer too, demanded sympathy for himself, as if he were the one suffering.

When they had dragged Sharpie through the crowd, the widow's heart-rending voice again rang out.

"Murderer!" she shouted and rushed toward Sharpie. "Who will feed my orphans? Murderer!"

They barely managed to restrain her, and confusion broke out in the crowd. The King raised his paw and everyone was silent. He then turned to her again.

"Your husband," he said, addressing the widow, "was our brother, despite our disagreements . . . We won't abandon you. Your children are my children."

"In what sense?" the Queen was alarmed.

"In the very highest," the King said and pointed to the sky. After that he pointed to the widow and turning to the royal treasurer, he ordered: "Roll out two heads of cabbage for her this time and give her one head daily, with the right to exchange it for a head of cauliflower, as soon as our experiments are completed, experiments we are observing and helping along . . . And now, rabbits, back to your burrows. Good night!''

On the treasurer's orders, they rolled out two heads of cabbage from the royal storehouse.

''My benefactor,'' the widow sobbed, falling with her head between both heads of cabbage and hugging them at the same time, so that no one could tear any pieces off.

''Our King's really a good guy,'' the rabbits said, wandering back to their burrows. Several of the females eyed Ponderer's widow in an envious, unwholesome way.

''Others have husbands, and after their deaths they get to take things home,'' one female said, poking her good-for-nothing husband in the side with her paw. ''And you're alive, just hopping around the jungle for nothing.''

''Dearie, during his lifetime, mine wasn't any better,'' the widow said unexpectedly boldly, trying to soothe her; and pushing both heads along, she rolled them to her burrow.

8

The next day a new herald was sent off to the Neutral Path. There he met with the Great Python's aides, who accompanied him to the Tsar's underground palace.

The Great Python was lying in a huge, damp, warm gallery of the underground palace, surrounded by his loyal aides and guards. His personal physician crept along his huge, extended body, observing the speed of rabbits moving along the Great Python's stomach. The underground palace was lit by phosphorescent lamps that provided an otherworldly light. Along the walls, stuffed examples of the more interesting hunting trophies (which the Great Python had been fortunate enough to swallow) were mounted.

The famous court sculptor of the boas could recreate, with total accuracy, the form of any animal swallowed, by following the outlines of the distended stomach of the boa who had swallowed the animal. Among the rabbits, wild goats, herons and monkeys, there was a stuffed Native in the Prime of His Life; after this native had been swallowed, with some difficulty, the Great Python had been chosen Tsar of the Boas.

The point was that hypnotizing and then swallowing a native was especially difficult, and if he had a quiver full of arrows sticking out from behind his back (and this one had had arrows), it was hellish torture.

Though this is a state secret, it should be revealed, however, that the Great Python didn't actually hypnotize his native. Rather, he bumped into him while the native was dead drunk. He was sleeping in the jungle under a chestnut tree, from which he'd been dipping wild honey from a hole in the trunk. He'd gotten so full of it that he'd crashed to the ground right there.

This still ordinary python did reveal his sharp wits, however, by not starting to swallow the native right there under the chestnut tree, where a ravaging swarm was still buzzing; instead, he dragged him deep into the jungle and swallowed him there. It took several days to do this, and the boas gathered round to observe the heroic swallowing of the Native in the Prime of His Life, as they later called that unfortunate glutton.

All the surrounding boas saw that he swallowed him fair and square. Only later did he tell them that he had hypnotized him.

With the passing of years, he forgot that the native had been dead drunk, and he sincerely thought that he had indeed hypnotized him. And that's not surprising. After all, he'd seen a sleeping native only once, and he'd heard about how he'd hypnotized this one hundreds of times, first from his own mouth, and later from others.

It must be said that certain of these outstanding swallowings, the sculpted commemorations of which were exhibited here, had been performed by other notable boas. But when the Great Python was named the Tsar of the Boas, for some reason he quarrelled with these notable boas, after which they disappeared, though the exhibits remained. And lest an outstanding feat in this area, which had educational significance, be lost, it became necessary to attribute it to the Great Python.

More precisely, it wasn't even necessary to attribute these outstanding swallows to him. His closest aides and advisors ascribed these feats to him directly.

"But after all, I didn't swallow that ostrich there," he objected feebly in such instances.

"But how many outstanding swallows did you perform before any sculptor could immortalize your deed?" his viziers and advisors objected strongly, and even caustically.

"That's true too," the Great Python agreed, and the next sculpted portrait of an outstanding swallow was attributed to the Great Python, and the next, like clockwork.

We should note another of this palace's wonders. There was a supply of live rabbits in one of its most subterranean rooms, in case of any natural disaster.

There were about a thousand rabbits there, preserved in a state of hypnosis. The rabbits lay in rows, deep in a lethargic sleep. Every morning and every evening, Fridge, one of the most fearsome members of the whole boa nation, slithered among them.

If one of the rabbits emerged from this state of hypnosis (and there were cases of this), then one look from Fridge was enough to make it sink back to sleep. Fridge saw to it that the rabbits didn't wake up and at the same time that they didn't slip from this lethargy into the eternal sleep of death, which in fact sometimes happened. It was also one of Fridge's duties to clean up after the dead rabbits. Even on the hottest days, the rabbits gave off an excellent coolness, which enveloped the Great Python's body.

The third wonder of this underground palace was the so-called treasure room. Here they brought all kinds of interesting objects, which had been found in the boas' feces. The boas, therefore, had a habit of attentively examing their own feces. Besides that, there was a law in the realm that boas who had swallowed natives were obliged to hand over any decorations and weapons which had not been digested.

As a matter of fact, the boas had long tried to maintain good relations with the natives. Every instance of a boa swallowing a native was officially condemned by the Great Python, that is, if the relatives or friends found out about it. It was stressed that if these items (which remained after the native had been swallowed) were returned to a relative with an expression of condolence, the native would be very satisfied and quickly get over the loss.

By the way, the ordinary boas could never fully understand whether the Great Python endorsed the digestion of natives or not. That is, in the depth of their souls (which in boas are located at the bottoms of their stomachs), they understood that he always supported this notion, but taking into consideration the interests of the whole nation, he would sometimes condemn a boa, even in a very cruel way. But on the other hand, the natives were always occupied with internecine warfare, and they frequently resorted to the boas for assistance, in order to take care of their enemies.

Usually in such cases, both sides conducted their negotiations through some monkey, trying to use extreme caution, and the monkey received as its reward the right to tear up the former owner's field on the first night of his absence, when no one yet knew about his demise.

It was possible to hire a suitable boa for the sum of five rabbits. The Great Python wouldn't have paid any attention to this if the higher interests of his nation didn't force him to take stern measures.

And if he himself had to speak with any natives, he usually ordered (out of a sense of tact) that the curtains be drawn in front of the sculpture of the Native in the Prime of His Life.

It's time, however, to return to the rabbits' herald, who was delivering his king's proposal to the Great Python, from time to time glancing at the appointments of the halls in the underground palace, which gave it a majestic, that is, ominous appearance.

The herald told about the conditions of Yearner's dash along a boa. As usual, and according to the rabbits' diplomatic custom, nothing was said directly. The King conveyed to his kind brother that if one of his quicker boas would kindly accept the proposal and would provide a mutually beneficial lesson, then both nations would profit from it, in both the physiological and psychological senses.

The herald also spoke about the scandalous behavior of the boa which had swallowed Ponderer.

He said that the boa in question, which had violated the inter-species agreement about the humane swallowing of a rabbit, had conducted mocking conversations with his prey, had applied torture in the form of caprice and uncertainty, and had finally refused to swallow the mortally tormented rabbit. The said rabbit had been so deranged by this torture that the unfortunate victim had been forced to throw himself into the boa's mouth. All this had happened, the herald added at the end, before the eyes of another rabbit, who was not prepared to maintain a vow of silence.

The Great Python heard all of this, thought a little, said:

"Convey on my behalf to your King that we are not natives, we do not arrange shows. And thank him for the communication about the unworthy behavior of the boa, he will be punished."

When the herald had left the room, the Great Python asked his chief vizier:

"What is this 'vow of silence'?"

"A nap in the afternoon," he answered, without even thinking. He was able to answer any question without thinking, and for this he had been named the Tsar's grand vizier.

"Gather the boas," the Great Python commanded. "I'm going to speak with my people. Ensure the presence of the one who swallowed Ponderer! Call all the adult boas. And the female boas, who are sitting on their eggs, they should be pulled off and driven here!"

At the appointed hour, the Great Python was lying in front of his coiled fellow tribesmen. He was waiting for them finally to find a comfortable position facing him. Several of them slithered up a fig tree, which grew in front of the palace, so they could see the Tsar better from there, and so that he could, if he wished, see them.

The Great Python, as usual, began his speech with the anthem. But this time his voice did not radiate cheerfulness and joy at seeing his nation, rather bitterness and anger.

"Descendants of the Dragon," he began, fastidiously eyeing the rows of boas.

"Glory's heirs, victors," he continued with bitterness, showing how the descendants were squandering their great heritage.

"Disciples of the Python!" he continued in a penetrating voice, overcoming his native hiss, showing that there was no greater shame than having such disciples.

"Young Boa Constrictors," he sighed with hopeless sarcasm.

"Disgrace! I have been disgraced!" the Great Python throbbed in well-elaborated hysterics.

This was followed by the rumbling, fidgeting, and hissing of sympathetic boa constrictors.

"What happened? We don't know about anything," they asked the boas on the periphery, who considered their lack of knowledge generally as a certain type of peripheral merit, that is, the lack of any bad knowledge.

"What happened!" the Great Python repeated with extraordinary bitterness. "I should ask you what's happened! Dear old boas, comrades in spilling blood — for what, I ask you, have you hypnotized legions of rabbits, swallowed them, and in whose name have you gotten immortal scars and wounds in your stomachs?

"Oh, Tsar," the old boas hissed, "in the name of our Great Dragon."

"My sisters," the Tsar turned to the female half, "maidens and mothers, with whom do you sleep and on whom do you sit, I ask you!"

"Oh, Tsar," the mothers and maidens answered, "we sleep with boas and we sit on eggs, from which young boas are born."

"Stubby," the Tsar shouted, "where's Stubby?"

"I'm here," Stubby said, moving away some branches and sticking his head out through the fig leaves. Lately he had preferred to attend the Tsar's meetings in the relative safety of the tree's branches.

"Oo-ooh!" the Tsar began to howl, looking for Stubby in the fig tree and failing to find words for his indignation. "Fig leaves, bananas . . .Degradation . . . Where's Squinter?"

"Oh Tsar," Squinter hissed pitifully, "elephants trampled me . . ."

Having thus prepared the boas' psyches, the Tsar told all those gathered around about the shameful behavior of the young boa while he was attempting to swallow Ponderer. While he was speaking, two guards dragged the young boa, who had been so unsuccessful at hunting and swallowing Ponderer, out of the crowd.

In his defense, he began to tell his now familiar story about how tired he had been, about how the mole had deceived him, and then he'd gotten lost, and how he'd seen two rabbits instead of the one he'd been promised, because he'd never heard rabbits could breed that fast.

The boas were indignant at the behavior of one of their former tribesmen.

"Why did you converse with it?" some of them asked him. "Didn't you know that silence must be maintained while swallowing a rabbit?"

"I knew that," the young boa (who was no longer little) replied. "But it was a very strange rabbit. I tried to hypnotize it, and it wiggled its ears, it sneezed in my face!"

"Well, so what?" the boas responded. "It sneezes — you swallow."

Then one of the peripheral boas moved forward and on behalf of all the peripheral boas, he expressed his indignation. He said that he'd had a totally analogous case, where he came across two rabbits when they were making love. It turned out, that unlike his former brother, he had personally not lost his self-assurance, he'd hypnotized both of them at once and swallowed them right then and there.

The boas listened to the story of this peripheral boa with deferential pleasure. Even the Tsar calmed down noticeably while he was listening to him. He had swallowed rabbits making love on more than one occasion, and so he decided to speak with that peripheral boa, face to face after the meeting, to find out in greater detail what sort of taste sensation he had experienced during that piquant time of swallowing.

"Pay attention to the experience of that boa way back there," the Tsar said, "he's talking about something very interesting here . . ."

The young boa tried to justify himself, saying that, unlike those rabbits, his hadn't been busy making love; on the contrary, they were thinking together, which is far from being the same thing.

"It's the same thing," the indignant boas hissed.

He made one last attempt to defend himself, counting on the notion that having deprived the rabbits of their wisest member, he had removed a leader and at the same time he had acquired that rabbit's wisdom.

"How much can anyone teach fools like you?" the Tsar shot back. "All wisdom has an intraspecific sense. Thus wisdom for the rabbits is stupidity for us . . . Please thank the peripheral boa for improving our mood with his story . . . We've decided not to deprive you of your life, but rather to banish you to the desert. You can feast on saxaul plants there, if you're such a vegetarian, and we'll let this serve as a lesson to Stubby . . .''

On the Great Python's signal, the boas began to slither away. The young boa was dragged away toward the desert by a convoy of two guards.

'' . . . A boa should rule over the boas,'' he heard the Tsar muttering behind him, ''and what am I to you, a piece of stinking log, is that what I am?''

9

Since that time several months had passed, maybe it was more like a year. No one really knows. The boa who had been banished from his tribe cursed his fate, and especially that herald, and now he had to slither over the burning sands in search of food.

Looking at his flaccid, wrinkled body, it would have been hard to say that just about a year ago he had been full of strength, a smallish boa with a lot of promise. No, now about all you could say about him was that he looked like a snake who was no longer young, that he'd lived a lot and poorly to boot.

Actually the moral torment, caused by his chronic hunger, had taken its toll.

He'd had to swear off the saxual from the very start because his stomach demanded, insisted on food with a more complex biological structure.

Several times he'd used Squinter's method to lure the eagles, which soared over the desert. But he'd paid too dearly by using this method under the desert conditions.

Lying for a long time in the sand, under the fiery sun, and not moving at all, was a terrible torment.

Once, having suffered a sunstroke, he barely came to and slithered over to the shade of a saxual. He decided then not to feign being dead any more. In general, he noticed that feigning death here in the desert was quite unpleasant. It was interesting to pretend to be dead when you were healthy and full of vigor, but when you were ill, a boa abandoned in the desert, it was awful to feign death, because it was too close to the truth.

In the end, he'd adapted to catching mice and lizards by a little oasis. Having dug down into the sand, he'd wait until the mice or lizards would take a drink. And then, if they passed by fairly close to him, he'd stick out his head and force them to freeze in terror, and then swallow them.

If they didn't come to the watering hole for a long time, he'd shake off the sand, drink some water and cool his burned skin in the water, and then he'd dig down again into that miserable sand.

Once Sharpie hopped over to this watering hole. He had changed tremendously from those distant times. His fur was in bad shape, he'd sliced his right ear on some cactus, and it had become forked, like a swallow's tail. His body was so emaciated that you could count every rib, which the boa, by the way, did automatically.

"Greetings to the traitor," he said, sticking his head out of the sand and shaking it.

Sharpie stopped lapping water and turned around.

"What kind of hermit boa do we have here?" the rabbit asked without any fear, looking at the boa. Unfortunately, bravery too often results from a feeling of not treasuring life, while cowardice always results from a false estimation of its worth.

Sharpie, by the way, had been banished to the desert before the young boa had been, and he didn't know anything about the boa's fate. In fact he'd never seen its face before.

"Don't you recognize me?" the Hermit Boa asked despondently, comprehending that he must have changed quite a bit during this period, and by no means for the better.

"I've not had the honor of meeting you," Sharpie replied indifferently; he was preparing to hop away, but he stopped because he was intrigued by the Hermit Boa's words.

"Because of you, I lost my native land, that is, the place where I used to have wonderful food," the boa hissed. "Because of your mean song, I went out to swallow Ponderer, and I ended up being banished to the desert."

"Oh, it's you, you lazybones," Sharpie said scornfully, "that's just what you deserved."

"I hate you, you damned traitor, more than anything else on the face of the earth!" the Hermit Boa said, looking at Sharpie with bitter hatred.

"But just imagine what happened to me," Sharpie responded. "Yes, I sinned, I betrayed a fellow rabbit. But you, you nitwit, you couldn't take proper advantage of my treachery, and you essentially deprived it of any sense. What could be lower in the eyes of a traitor than not having any one who can make proper use of the treachery?"

"I hate you," the Hermit Boa repeated, "you, you. You pushed me into that misguided temptation . . ."

"I spit on your hatred," Sharpie said. "There's no place to graze here in the desert, and so I have a lot of time with nothing to do but ponder . . ."

"And so what have you thought up, you scoundrel?" the boa inquired, moving slightly closer to him.

"Lots of things," Sharpie replied, not paying any attention to the boa's movements. "Now I understand the secret of treachery. After all, my people did consider me a Sharpie. At first I thought that this whole affair had been caused by the unlucky cabbage leaf, which I had promised the Queen to dry for a keepsake, but then I couldn't restrain myself on the road and ate half of it. Then I understood that I really didn't want to leave the royal table. And then I thought of the most important thing. The trap concealed in every treacherous act, when it's been formulated but not yet carried out, is in the duality of your situation."

"What do you mean by duality?" the boa asked and moved even closer to Sharpie; in his mind he was squeezing Sharpie's ribs sweetly with the muscles of his stomach.

"This is what I mean by duality," Sharpie went on, seemingly inspired. "Having decided to betray someone, you already imagine all those riches promised by the treachery. I felt I was the proud possessor of the freshest cabbage, the greenest beans, the sweetest peas, not to speak about such trifles as carrots. And all of this without even having done the nefarious deed; notice that this is where the base deception lies!

"In my dreams I seemed to have gone through with the treachery, stolen all the blessings from my fate, and without actually having betrayed anyone I'd returned to my position of an honest rabbit. And until I had actually carried it out, the joy of feeling that I'd tricked fate, that I'd mentally stolen all the blessings of the treachery, without having paid for them at all, was so great that it whipped aside any thought about possible future remorse. That's how we're created! We can be happy about joys we haven't yet experienced, but we can't feel the pangs of conscience because of some planned betrayal. And even if we can, it's a thousand times weaker. That's right.

"How did all this come about? It seemed that I had committed the treacherous act in my mind, but it was nothing, I could still go on living. And so that must mean there was nothing special in the treachery itself. And I just couldn't connect this feeling that the treacherous act was no big deal, with the notion that this arose because I hadn't actually done the deed! Do you understand how cunning fate can be?

"In order to push us toward evil, the devil eases any

terror of him by offering the possibility of not doing any-
thing evil, the possibility of playing with it. You know, the
devil says, I'm not forcing you to do evil, I simply think
you don't have the right opinion about it. That's not evil,
he says, that's sober accounting, that's an opportunity to
get rid of stupid prejudice. In any case, get acquainted with
your future relationship, talk with it, rehearse it, and if you
don't like all this, you don't have to do anything about it.
That's where we're trapped. While we're playing with evil,
it's still not an evil act that's been committed (our silly con-
sciousness says to us), but in fact an evil deed has been
done, because by playing with evil, we have already lost
our sacred fastidiousness, which nature bestowed on us.

"That's why traitors are always paid in advance, and
they're always paid shamefully little! But after all, they could
be paid even less! Because no matter how little is paid, be-
fore the actual betrayal the person considers this payment
pure profit: so whether he does it or not, the money's al-
ready his, and the joy too. So once again, if you're happy,
then there must be nothing special about the future betrayal
itself, otherwise, where would this joy come from . . .?"

"That's too subtle for me," the Hermit Boa interrupt-
ed him. "For example, I swallowed the wisest rabbit and
I still don't quite get what you're driving at . . ."

"Then listen some more," Sharpie went on, turning
his soul inside out. "Now you understand that it's impos-
sible to turn back. Your soul is tainted, and because of that
the payment now seems too low. You sense the terrible in-
justice that has been done to you. Yes, to you and only you,
and not to the one you betrayed! You feel hatred for him.
He allowed himself to be betrayed, and therefore he
betrayed you. He sort of becomes a participant in the de-
ception.

"And how does it turn out, Hermit? You'd hoped to
the very end that you'd be able to carry it off, that you could
race back. At the very worst, you could cut out the tainted

piece of your soul and give it to the treachery, and you could keep the rest for yourself. After all, you didn't agree to give your whole soul to the traitorous deed, otherwise you wouldn't have made such an agreement!

"It's hard for boas to grasp this, but we rabbits are warm-blooded and cleanly by nature. I'd compare a rabbit's soul with a pure white tablecloth. I dreamed of eating clean, royal cabbage, beans, and peas on precisely that pure tablecloth in the future. What about the treachery? I knew that it wouldn't help to decorate my snow-white tablecloth, but I thought I could tear off a piece of it, the part spoiled by the treachery, and I'd spread the rest out, so that I could enjoy the blessings of life. And so what happened? Whoops! The whole tablecloth fell into the shit! How could I have understood that? Where was I going to eat my cabbage, and green beans and peas that I'd earned? Answer me! What had I been dreaming about? That I'd eat off a clean tablecloth and toss scraps from it to the poor rabbits, all the while grumbling at the idlers. Oh, what happiness that was going to be — grumbling about those lazy rabbits and the overly fastidious ones too, all the while tossing them crumbs from my own generous table!

"And so now what happened? I have to eat alone on a shitty tablecloth! It turns out that treachery smears the whole tablecloth with its shit, not just a part of it, as I'd thought. So, did that mean I didn't know it? It turns out that they paid me nothing, there's nothing left for me but my shit-covered tablecloth, off of which I'm forced to eat its shitty produce.

"Who can guess how much a rabbit with a tainted soul feels like an orphan? After all, we rabbits are clean and warm-blooded creatures. Oh, I felt it there in the jungle right away, although not as clearly as I do now. Even those stinking marmosets began to scorn me. Spite — that's what I had left then. And the most spiteful spite for those rabbits who were clean! Why didn't you stop me, if you're so wonderful, I thought."

"Oh, you're just talking nonsense!" the Hermit Boa interrupted him. "Even before I swallowed the wisest rabbit, I could have told you what stupid things you were saying. Who could have stopped you if you'd never told anyone about your treachery? Still, you're a real bastard! You've woven all these words in order to hide their true substance. The fact is that you're a warm-blooded rabbit who's betrayed a brother, that means you spilled the blood of a warm-blooded rabbit. No, I think I should swallow you. Even though I don't have the same strength as before, and the heat interferes with my hypnosis, I feel my hatred for you will help . . ."

"Don't scare me too much," Sharpie replied. "You know, I still believe that Ponderer was right about the hypnosis."

"Don't speak about that, reptile!" the Hermit Boa shouted in extreme anger, feeling this fury contracting and releasing all the muscles of his body. "You betrayed him and now you want to make use of his discovery?"

"I'm not doing any such thing," Sharpie said wanly. "The fact is that I don't believe in anything on earth now, and that means I can't believe in your hypnosis. So you can stare at me as much as you want with your peepers!"

"Ooh, I hate you so much!" the Hermit hissed, feeling the muscles of his body contract and loosen. "And I feel that my hatred is giving birth to some rather fruitful thoughts . . ."

"A boa, giving birth to a thought?" Sharpie smiled ironically, looking at the hermit with boredom in his eyes, "that's because it's too hot for you . . ."

"No, no," the Hermit repeated, coiling impatiently, "I feel with my whole body that I'm giving birth to a new thought. It seems to me . . . I'm not certain . . . It seems to me that I could suffocate you in a new way . . ."

"Do you have in mind your foul breath?" Sharpie asked. "You should remember that you're too late . . . A rabbit who bears a bad smell in his soul . . ."

"No, no!" the boa shouted, coiling in extreme agitation. "My hatred is giving birth to some strange love . . . An austere love without any tenderness . . . I feel an uncontrollable urge to squeeze you in an embrace . . ."

With these words, the Hermit Boa coiled around the rabbit in one movement and began to choke him in a clumsy and awkward way.

"Leave me alone," Sharpie tried to get away from the boa, still not quite grasping what this crazy boa was trying to do. "Let me loose, I don't want your slimy embrace . . . First of all, I'm not a female boa . . . It hurts . . . I'm not even a female rabbit . . . What kind of perversion is this . . .?"

"Just wait," the boa muttered, curling around Sharpie, "just one more coil. We'll stick the head . . . One more knot . . . Tighter . . . Tighter . . ."

"I hate all of you!" Sharpie managed to scream before he lost consciousness in the boa's fatal embrace.

"Oof," the boa exhaled, "I'm so tired it seems like I wasn't smothering it, but the other way around . . . But it's not surprising — this is the first time in the world that a boa has captured anything without hypnosis . . . The Great Python will take me back because of this brilliant discovery, he'll hug me in a big embrace . . . Although now that sounds like it could have double meaning . . . Now I'm going to regain my strength and then go back to the other boas . . . We'll see who's the most worthy to become the next Tsar of the Boas . . ."

With these words he proceeded to swallow the rabbit. Thus Sharpie's life ended. He'd had a lot of abilities; unfortunately, he'd loved the royal table more than his abilities. He'd been admitted to it but, alas, at too high a cost.

10

Meanwhile, during Sharpie and Hermit's exile, important events had taken place in the boas' realm, and in the rabbits' kingdom, too. Ponderer's discovery about hypnosis, and Yearner's promise to run the length of a boa and back in many ways destroyed the relations between the rabbits and boa constrictors that had been built up over the centuries.

A huge number of anarchically inclined rabbits had appeared; they either didn't go along with the old notion about hypnosis, or they did, but only slightly. A large number of boas were on starvation diets. Some of them became so nervous because of their meager rations that they started and turned around at the slightest touch, thinking that perhaps a rabbit wanted to run alongside. One boa even bolted when a little old walnut fell on him unexpectedly.

Even more ominous reports came in from the peripheral boas. There the authority of the boas had fallen so low that instances were observed of monkeys urinating on boas who were resting under trees. It's true that they did it from a fairly respectable height, and they later apologized, explaining that they had done it out of absentmindedness. But it was difficult to comprehend why there had never been instances of such purposeful absentmindedness before.

"We cannot solve that problem separately," the Great Python said in response to the complaints of the peripheral boas. "We will decide on it only after we have bolstered the status of hypnosis . . . And for now, follow the example of your fellow boa, the one who swallowed a loving couple . . ."

That's how the Great Python responded, but it was rather cold comfort. And what could he do, expecially since the rabbits' disgraceful shouting could sometimes be heard right next to his underground palace?

The effectiveness of hypnosis diminished catastrophically. In order to evoke a fighting spirit in the boas (because it was dying out), the Great Python ordered those boas living fairly close to his palace to come every day, before they went out hunting, to familiarize themselves with his hunting trophies. The outlying boas had to slither over in large groups once a month. But this not only didn't help, in fact, it made the boas even more furious.

"That was just the way it used to be," they said and crept off despondently into the jungle.

And the devil only knows what the rabbits started doing! Sometimes they sped away right at the very height of the hypnosis, or they began to conduct mocking negotiations during the hypnosis, saying something like: What'll I get out of this, if I let myself be swallowed, and so forth.

One rabbit, which had already quieted down during hypnosis, and had already sunk into a hypnotic nirvana, suddenly winked at a boa, even though its eye was fatally tired. The boa, stuck by this new medical twist, stopped the ritual and looked at the rabbit. Then the boa decided that he was just imagining it, then returning to the ritual of hypnosis, he lowered his head, again fixing his unblinking eyes on the rabbit. The rabbit was completely motionless, his eyes seemed to be sweetly tired, but as soon as the boa wanted to open his mouth, the rabbit winked at him again, as if it wanted to say something important. The boa broke off the hypnosis again, but the rabbit once more sat motionless and inert before him.

Apparently, I'm just imagining this, the boa thought, and again started the hypnosis. And the same thing was repeated. The rabbit's dying eye winked cockily at the boa at the last possible moment. Finally, the sixth or seventh time, the boa couldn't take it any more and as soon as the rabbit winked at him, he tried to catch it with his mouth, but the rabbit unexpectedly soared up like roman candle, turned a somersault, and hopped away.

What did it mean to say with that? the boa thought,

it's not possible that there wasn't some reason for doing that.

He searched for that rabbit for several days to find out why it had been winking at him. He decided that the rabbit had wanted to communicate some important secret to him, but he had remained true to tradition (old boa that he was), and he'd decided not to converse during the trapping. Now he'd decided that no matter what he was going to find that rabbit and find out from it what had been going on.

Finally, he caught sight of his rabbit near a blackberry bush, which it was casually gnawing on. Without even trying to hypnotize it, he reminded it about himself and asked why it had been winking at him during the hypnosis.

"Just wanted to," the rabbit said, putting blackberry leaf in its mouth, "I just wanted to be naughty, to have some fun."

"Have some fun?! During hypnosis?!" The old boa exclaimed, and he died right then, stunned by the general lowering of moral standards.

Another boa suffered a shameful humiliation. A charming, plump female rabbit made him lose his mind, because instead of winking, she would come to at the last minute of the hypnosis and then hop away.

She tormented him from morning to noon, and finally, twitching her plump sides coquettishly in front of him, she said:

"Steal a head of cabbage from the natives; then I'll eat my fill and give myself to you . . ."

They agreed that the boa would creep back to the same spot with a head of cabbage. Excited and in a rush, the boa slithered to the nearest village, crept into a garden, and tore off a head of cabbage there, but when he tried to shove the head through a hole in the wattle fence, he was discovered by the natives and given a sound thrashing.

In fact, the idiot had tried to stick the cabbage through

a hole that was smaller than the circumference of the cabbage. Thinking that all bodies have the same characteristics as those of snakes — such as being able to ooze themselves through any opening — he went mad when he saw that the cabbage wouldn't go through the hole. He was so incensed and made the wattles crack so loudly that the natives heard him.

When they caught him doing this, they beat him half to death with sticks. The natives, whose minds didn't differ much from those of the boas, decided that they'd killed him and so they left him hanging on the fence to scare off other boas. Later, laughing at his slow-wittedness, they closed up the hole in the fence, picked up the head of cabbage, wiped it off a little, and ate it right there. At night the battered boa came to and slithered off into the jungle.

The boas and the natives had always had fairly decent relations. Keeping in mind that the rabbits were the ones who tore up their gardens, and that the boas served to keep the rabbit population down, the natives treated the boas with respect, although in deference to the other inhabitants of the jungle, they never stressed this fact.

What's more, sometimes they joined the protests organized by the jungle's inhabitants in regard to boas swallowing their prey in an especially cruel manner — for example, when they swallowed female rabbits in full view of a bunny, or vice versa.

In some truly rare cases, if a boa had managed to swallow a doddering old native or some infant who had wandered into the jungle, the leader of the natives sent his man to the Great Python to complain, invariably pointing out that the crime had been committed while the monkeys had been watching.

The Great Python received him in his quarters at the palace with all honors due him, and the stuffed Native in the Prime of His Life was characteristically curtained off with banana leaves in a gesture of diplomatic tact.

The Great Python invariably promised to get to the bottom of the matter and punish the guilty party, each time returning to the stranger undigested objects which had been found in the accused boa's feces: a leather talisman, beads, bracelets, a bronze hatchet, or a piece of spear with a bone tip.

The Great Python returned all these items to the King's envoy, so that he could pass along the objects to the relatives of the victim, with an expression of most sincere condolence and a promise to punish the guilty party. Then, if they happened to be speaking about a man, the Great Python nodded at the pieces of his weapon, which had passed through the boa, and said:

"We'll punish the guilty party, although he's already been punished quite a bit."

It's interesting to note that the natives' leader decided not to investigate those instances when the natives had perished without the monkeys noticing it; he did this out of considerations of prestige. It was thought that the boas didn't dare touch the natives, and the attacks were explained by saying that some boa had confused a native with a monkey.

It's true that this time the leader's envoy had objected to the odd attempt of the boa to carry off a head of cabbage, and this provoked a most decisive protest.

The Great Python shared the indignation of the natives' leader in the most sincere way. He decided that it must have been Stubby, who was continuing his degeneration, and finally he'd become like the rabbits and the monkeys.

"The boas are now experiencing some temporary difficulties," the Great Python said to the leader's envoy, "but a boa stealing cabbage — that's never happened and never will happen. We have one degenerate among us called Stubby; he's always brought shame upon himself and continues to disgrace our nation. Hunt him with dogs, beat him with sticks. All we'll say is thank you for doing it."

"I'll pass that information along," the envoy said and then left. When he reached the village, he told the leader about everything he'd heard and added that, personally speaking, the boas just weren't the same as usual.

And indeed the boas weren't their normal selves. The monkeys told an amusing anecdote about the boas all over the jungle. It seems that one monkey had seen a sparrow landing on a coiled boa, thinking that it was a pile of elephant shit. They say this impudent little sparrow pecked at it several times, then chirped: "Just like shit, but it's something else," and flew away.

And even if this incident hadn't taken place, the mere possibility of spreading such an anecdote gave witness to the unprecedented decline in the boas' prestige.

Yes, the boas indeed weren't their normal selves then. Things had even gone so far that the Tsar's best hunters began to miss their targets. Usually they would move out for a royal hunt, and having hypnotized a rabbit, they made it known that the prey was ready to be consumed.

The Great Python then slithered over with his suite, and if the rabbit seemed sufficiently appetizing to him, he consumed it himself, and if he found it not to his liking, he left it for his suite.

But now it wasn't possible to maintain the suite as before. The suite had to avail themselves of the meager rations from the Tsar's refrigerator; they couldn't hunt for themselves because they had long ago lost the ability to work with a rabbit that wasn't already stunned.

The day the Hermit Boa returned to the jungle, the Great Python had gone without breakfast for the first time in his long reign. It's true that one of the Tsar's hunters had managed to hypnotize a fairly respectable rabbit. He then slithered off to the side, but when the Tsar approached his prey, the rabbit suddenly started and ran away.

"Thanks for the breakfast," was all the Tsar could say, looking at his hunter.

"You could have been a mite quicker," the hunter responded audaciously, and the Tsar, silently swallowing the insult (instead of the rabbit), slithered away to his underground palace.

There a boa, which had been sent early in the morning to conduct secret negotiations with the King of the rabbits, was waiting. The Great Python had informed the King that such an acute disturbance in the balance of nature would most certainly lead to unfortunate consequences, not only for the boas, but also for the rabbits themselves, not to speak about the other inhabitants of the jungle. In this regard, he asked the King to keep his rabbits within the bounds of the good, old traditions.

"So, what did he say to you?" the Great Python asked his envoy, trying to stifle the sucking pangs of his bottomless stomach with a hungry yawn. Every once in a while he looked over his stuffed hunting trophies, which for a moment seemed to him like freshly hypnotized rabbits, or graceful wild goats, or well-formed herons.

"In the name of the Dragon, cover them up," he moaned, unable to bear this torment, "if someone's here . . . Impossible to work like that . . ."

And only after all the trophies had been covered with banana leaves did he continue his conversation with the emissary.

"So, what did he tell you?" the Great Python asked, already seeing by the sour expression on his envoy's face that he shouldn't expect anything positive.

"He says that he's barely able to stay in power himself," the envoy replied, "only because of the cauliflower . . ."

"What?" the Great Python asked. "They're not obeying him either?"

"No," the envoy responded. "He says that every morning, when they give the report about the effective distance of the hypnosis, the rabbits openly laugh . . ."

"I see," the Great Python nodded gloomily. "Well, okay, you're free to go now . . ."

It's worth mentioning that during this period, even the highly inflated figures put out by the royal chancellery made it obvious that the curve of rabbits who perished in the mouths of boas had dropped sharply.

No matter how much the royal propaganda exaggerated the number of rabbits which had died (now the propagandists affirmed that the boas on the whole were currently hunting in the deepest, darkest corners of the jungle in the rabbit kingdom, where cases of cruel double swallowings of loving couples had been observed), still the rabbits couldn't help but understand that the boas just weren't themselves now.

The rabbits, along with many of their relatives and their acquaintances, often broke off the hypnosis by sheer force of will, and some of them did everything we have already observed, or something like it.

The incident of the two rabbits being swallowed together, which as we know actually took place, was truly scandalous, but the propagandists overworked it to the point that many rabbits stopped believing that it had in fact taken place.

At first, they had told the rabbits what was known about this dastardly act. Seeing that they were outraged and rather distressed by this atrocity, the morning information began to give "New Details about the Peripheral Boa's Atrocity" each week.

Finally, in one of the latest reports, "From the Scene of the Tragedy," a rabbit on foot had brought news that the couple, it seems, had begged the boa to turn away and not to hypnotize them, at least not until the end of their first (and, alas) final intimacy. But it turned out that the merciless boa didn't want to listen to them, and so the couple made the heroic decision to remain in an embrace to the very end, and if they died physically in the boa's jaws, they would at least triumph ideologically.

"How did he learn about all of these details?" the rabbits began to doubt.

"What do you mean," the rabbit answered his doubters, "the monkeys were there, they saw and heard everything, and they told us . . ."

"Even the fact that it was their first time together?"

"Even that detail," he replied.

"Still, it's hard to believe," the rabbits said, knowing about their fellow rabbits' love for purity and the impossibility of their telling their executioner, that is the boa, about these things.

"You are not going to be permitted to sully the bright image of this couple in love," the King said, looking at the crowd of rabbits and trying to note those who doubted. They didn't try very hard to conceal themselves, though they also didn't want to stick out too much either.

The complexity of this historical moment was intensified by the fact that the rabbits actually withstood the boas' gaze rather often (under the influence of Ponderer's teachings and Yearner's never-ending attempts to instill them in their consciousness), which in turn was reflected in their decreasing measure of respect for the King personally, and for his rule as well.

But, on the other hand, the rabbits didn't want Yearner to attain total victory, because then they would have to leave the natives' gardens alone. They liked their life as it was: obeying the King a little, carrying out Ponderer's wishes a little, submitting to hypnosis as rarely as possible, and visiting the natives' gardens as often as possible.

The rabbits naughtily averted their eyes when Yearner hinted frequently about rising up against the King, and they said that they were not politically conscious enough for that.

"Why are you in such a hurry, work on us some more," they said. And Yearner continued to work on them, because there was nothing else for him to do, and all signs indicated that time was destroying the King's rule.

Yes, time was truly working against the King. He felt it himself day and night, when the Queen would jab him in the side and say:

"Think of something!"

"What can I think of?" the King replied, rubbing his side.

"Then there was no reason to banish Sharpie," the Queen replied angrily and turned her back to the King.

Actually, what could he think of? The main remedy — their fear of the boas — was growing weaker with every passing day. Sometimes the hypnosis misfired. There were masses of boa corpses in the jungle: they had starved to death. And the instances of boas seizing overly daring rabbits without using hypnosis were too rare and unreliable.

Once, during the normal information session for rabbits, six birds of prey flew right over the Royal Meadow, carrying the body of some large boa in their talons.

This sight was rather gruesome, especially from the point of view of those Admitted to the Table — those silent, large birds, that boa hanging lifelessly from their talons. It seemed that these symbolic birds were carrying away the last boa constrictor.

"Let a storm burst forth over the world!" the Poet shouted suddenly, apparently taking these birds for stormy petrels.

"Our Poet has really gone crazy," the King said, eyeing the Poet closely. The Poet was smiling radiantly, looking at the birds and greeting them with an outstretched paw.

Indeed, the Poet had been behaving rather stupidly lately. The fact is that the bunny with the good eyes, who had been assigned to him, had disappeared somewhere, and now the Poet took not only crows for stormy petrels, but even normal parrots, which caused the ordinary rabbits to split their sides laughing.

Now, seeing these birds carrying the boa, the ordinary rabbits let out such a squeal of joy that five of the birds were

frightened and let go, but one continued to grip the sway-
ing, vertical body. The stubborn bird which continued to
hold the boa flew lower and lower, because of the weight,
but then the other birds flew over to it, and taking hold of
the boa, they began to gain height.

It's true that the Wise Old Rabbit, who had been com-
manded to divine the significance of this sight, said that
despite the ominous appearance, it boded well for the
future.

"Why?" the King asked incredulously.

"A falling boa was again raised to the necessary
height," the Wise Old Rabbit said with assurance, because
now he was acting with certainty: if the boas came around,
then the grateful King would elevate him because of his mar-
vellous prediction, but if the boas sank into total debility,
then the King wouldn't have anything to worry about.

By the way, one extremely unpleasant bit of nonsense
was added to all these serious difficulties. A very tiny, but
already quite noxious bunny began to appear in the king-
dom of the rabbits, even in the area immediately surround-
ing the royal palace.

Once, when the King was strolling with his suite in the
well-protected part of the jungle which bordered on the roy-
al palace, the tiny bunny suddenly popped out of the bushes
and said sadly:

"Unca King, me want cau'flower . . ."

The Chief of the Guards and the King's retinue froze
in indignation. Only the King didn't lose his composure;
on the contrary, he seemed to come to life.

"Oh, my dear little bunny," he said, smiling and ap-
proaching the bushes where the bunny's sad face had ap-
peared. "We don't have any cauliflower yet, but we'll have
some very soon, because we're personally keeping track of
the experiments and helping wherever we can . . . But for
now the Queen will give you a treat — a fresh leaf of nice
green cabbage . . . It's good too . . ."

"Unca King, me want cau'flower . . ."

The King, trying to conceal his awkwardness, spread his arms as if to say, we have to be happy with what we've got, and he moved on. His retinue trailed after, having come back to life again; the male half of the suite began to talk about the breakdown in morals, which had even begun to appear among the little bunnies. The female half was more dissatisfied with other females who thought it was enough just to give birth to a bunny, and not to think at all about its upbringing.

Gradually the King and his suite calmed down and were in an even better mood than before they'd met the bunny. The King's mood improved because he had displayed his gentleness and condescension in regard to that audacious bunny, and the rabbits in his suite felt better because they had been unexpectedly diverted by the sight of the King caught off guard.

And then suddenly, on the way back, not far from the Royal Meadow, that same bunny popped out from the bushes again, and it repeated its request with inexpressible sadness:

"Unca King, me want cau'flower."

"Who do you think you're talking to?!" the Chief of the Royal Guards shouted; he had been the first to recover from the shock.

"Hooligan!" the court rabbits shouted. "Its parents should be brought in!"

"We have to know who's behind this!" the Queen exclaimed, winking at the Chief of the Guards and giving him another cabbage leaf.

The Chief of the Guards took the leaf and began to tread softly, approaching the bushes where the bunny's face had appeared, blinking its big, sad eyes. It seemed to be listening for something that it didn't hear, looking for something that didn't appear.

"Where do you live, my dear little bunny?" the Chief

of the Guards asked, bending over the bush like a father, trying with his whole pose to demonstrate the complete lack of military intentions on his part.

The bunny silently continued to listen for something that was never heard, continued to look for something that never appeared.

"Do you have a daddy and a mommy?"

A long, sad silence ensued.

"Here, I'm going to give you this cabbage leaf," the Chief of the Guards said in his tenderest voice, "and then you can tell me which nice rabbit sent you here to beg for cauliflower from Uncle King, okay?"

And without waiting for any sign of agreement, he held out the leaf for the bunny to take.

"Me want cau'flower," it said, just as sadly, though it took the cabbage leaf extended to it.

Again there was a long, painful silence.

But suddenly they heard the rustling of some unknown rabbit during this painful silence. He was crossing the path quite close to the King and his suite. He looked at them in a very unfriendly way, muttered something spiteful about Certain Rabbits, who were such gluttons, and a bunny who couldn't get even a leaf of cauliflower, and then he disappeared into the tall grass of the savannah. And what was especially insulting, when he entered the tall grass, he deliberately pushed the stalks of grass away from his face, showing his annoyance and unconcern about how he had publicly offended the King.

Without saying a word, the King turned and began to go toward the palace, his suite stretching out behind him.

"Seize him!" the Chief of the Guards finally shouted, having regained his senses.

"Which one do you mean?" one of the guards asked, not knowing whom he had in mind — the bunny or the unknown rabbit who had crossed the path.

"All of them!" the Chief of the Guards shouted, which

completely confused his guards, because part of their group was running after the suite. And while they were being brought back, the tracks of their brother rabbits had cooled. It was possible to understand why these rabbits had been seized, because everyone knew that the Chief of the Guards dreamed day and night about a conspiracy among those Admitted to the Table. They decided that he had finally uncovered this conspiracy.

Remembering that the Poet had a bunny guide to run alongside him, the Chief of the Guards decided to find out if this had been the bunny which had asked so insolently for the cauliflower during the King's stroll. He called the Poet over to him, but the Poet couldn't say anything that made much sense, although he had been in the King's suite at the time.

"I don't know," the Poet said, "I didn't see the bunny. I usually look up at the sky."

"Well, if we catch him, will you recognize him?" the Chief of the Guards asked, barely concealing his hatred for the Poet.

"I don't know," the Poet said, "I usually never looked at him, I was usually looking at the sky."

"Okay, you can go," the Chief of the Guards said, barely restraining himself. He had dreamed so often about hanging the Poet by his ears someday, and forcing him to be a little closer to his beloved sky that way, the sky he never took his eyes off of. But alas, the King for some reason felt that it was necessary to defend his court poet.

"If that imp is my guide," the Poet suddenly began to speak, "then a lot of things would be clear."

"What exactly?" the Chief of the Guards livened up a bit.

"Now it's clear that he used my poor eyesight to pretend that stormy petrels were crows. Oh, how many exhausted warriors I could have encouraged with my poetic voice, but they flew aimlessly above me!" the Poet exclaimed bitterly.

"For God's sake, go away!" the Chief of the Guards said, "otherwise, instead of seeing a stormy petrel, your wife will be confronted by a harbinger of grief!"

"No, I don't need any harbingers of grief," the Poet said and hastened to the exit.

Hardly able to settle down to normal business after talking with the Poet, the Chief of the Guards met with the King. He tried to justify the unforeseen incident during the stroll by saying that at first he'd taken the rabbit crossing the path for one of the guards, who just dressed differently, and then his aides had blundered.

"All I ask from you," the King said, "is a little bit of peace and quiet in the jungle when I stroll."

"You'll have it, Sire," the Chief of the Guards said significantly, "and we'll catch the criminal."

"We'll see," the King said and added, "have you heard any new rumors going around the kingdom?"

"I've heard some," the Chief of the Guards replied, "but we'll give out some of our own counterrumors."

"How?"

"It's rather complicated, Sire, but it has been established precisely that the same rabbits take pleasure in both rumors and counterrumors."

"Now you see who I'm forced to rule over," the King said, shaking his head.

"Now you see who I have to protect you from," the Chief of the Guards said.

"That's true too," the King said, and added, as a sign that the conversation was over, "well, go out there and keep your eyes peeled."

11

In fact, some ugly rumors had been spread around the kingdom. Some said that a wandering bunny had accidentally come across a catered banquet, where as usual the rabbits were stuffing themselves with all kinds of delicacies, including cauliflower.

It seemed that the bunny saw from the bushes how they were eating and drinking, but after they'd stuffed themselves till they couldn't eat any more, they began to feed the leftover cauliflower to the monkeys. The bunny couldn't take it any longer; he stepped out of the bushes, stuck out his paw and said:

"Unca King, me want cau'flower."

"Scram, you damned spy!" the King apparently said, and the guards chased that bunny so hard that they're still looking for him, and no one's been able to find him.

"Did they really feed others, those monkeys, and not spare any for their own bunny?" one of the listeners usually asked at this point.

"The important thing isn't that they couldn't show some kindness," the storyteller replied, "they just don't like it when ordinary rabbits see how they sit around a tablecloth which is all spotted with cauliflower juice."

"What do they do . . . smear it with cauliflower juice?" one of the listeners asked, noisily swallowing his saliva.

"They say it melts in your mouth, like nectar from flowers," the storyteller replied, "but while you're carrying it to your mouth, they say, it can smear, because the tenderest vegetables can't stand to be touched in a rough way."

"I would have put it in my mouth," one of the listeners said dreamily, "its colorful juice would have oozed out right under the roof of my mouth . . ."

And then all the rabbits, including the storyteller, stopped still and imagined (noisily swallowing their saliva) how this tender vegetable would melt in the mouth of that rabbit with the sweet tooth.

Another version had it that when the bunny asked for the cauliflower, the King (because he was a terrible penny-pincher) began to question the royal treasurer about the garden taxes the bunny's father had paid while he was alive — this rabbit had, by the way, perished in the mouth of a boa constrictor. After the treasurer had checked, he made it clear that the late rabbit hadn't paid much respect to the garden tax while he'd been alive and kicking. The unhappy bunny was left standing there, its tiny paw outstretched, for those Admitted to the Table to laugh at.

"Well, okay," the rabbits waxed indignant, "even if his parent didn't have much respect for the garden tax, what about the bunny? The King calls himself the father of all the bunnies."

The most interesting thing, however, was that these same rabbits also repeated the counterrumors, spread by the Chief of the Guards, with the same curiosity and sympathy.

According to one of these, it seemed that a rabbit had actually wandered into an extraordinarily secret planatation deep in the jungle, which was personally supervised by the King; with his guidance the rabbits of science, working together with the natives, were raising cauliflower. And then, it seemed, the bunny had seen a good-sized head in a vegetable bed, radiating all the colors of the rainbow, and it had asked:

"Unca King, me want cau'flower."

And in fact the natives and some of the scientists, who had been torn away from their work, did try to chase the bunny away (it seems it had only gotten lost). But the King, it seemed, had learned that the bunny was an orphan; he tore off the juiciest leaf from a ripe head of cauliflower, gave it to the bunny, and said:

"Very soon all orphans will be eating cauliflower."

"It'd be interesting to have a look at the little bunny who lucked out," the rabbits said after they'd heard this pleasant story.

"It's impossible to see it," the storyteller said significantly, "because it's now been hidden away — it knows the location of the plantation.

"Ah, of course," the rabbits easily agreed with this explanation, and by doing so they were perhaps hinting that they were in on something secret too. In general, rabbits very much liked being hush-hush about things. It seemed to them that rabbits who had been secreted away were swallowed by boas only in extreme cases.

By the way, Ponderer's widow once heard this version. It had been told in a circle of esteemed rabbits, by one who worked for the Royal Gurads. And that night she couldn't fall asleep for a long time. The King's statement, about all orphans being able to eat cauliflower soon, didn't give her any peace. She decided that now was the time to remind the King about his promise, that as soon as possible he would replace the welfare ration of cabbage with an equal amount of cauliflower.

She appeared at the palace early the next morning, joining the other esteemed widows who were waiting to receive their allotments. In all, there were about a dozen female rabbits, and all of them were frightfully jealous of each other, though by rights Ponderer's widow was considered the first among equals.

"Mine's still o-o-over there! When he was thinking . . ." she said, getting ready to raise a scandal if the treasurer didn't give her the cauliflower.

The widows, who sighed from time to time, just like widows, were standing and waiting for the storehouse to open. Now they were jealously holding their breath.

"What are you looking for?" the treasurer asked her, rolling the two heads of regular cabbage onto the counter.

"For the cauliflower," the widow replied, silently pushing the two heads of ordinary cabbage away from her.

"I've never seen any at all," the treasurer said, putting the heads on a shelf. "If you can, go to the King and ask him."

"I will," Ponderer's widow replied, listening to the other widows' grumblings; they were avowing, not too certainly, that they weren't any worse off as widows.

"You're worse off," she responded firmly, adding while she was leaving, "your husbands used to stuff themselves at the royal table, while mine thought day and night about the future."

Since they were already rather afraid of her, the widows were silent. For the same reason, she was able to pass without hindrance to the Royal Chancellery, where she threw open the door, started to sob, and went into the King's study:

She threw herself on the King's chest, and with the boldness permitted only for patriotic tears, she sobbed, repeating the same thing over and over (which annoyed the King):

"If he could get up . . . If he could see . . . If he could get up . . ." Finally, having calmed down, she reminded the King about substituting cauliflower for cabbage, and referred to the story she'd heard about the bunny.

"All of this is terribly exaggerated, my dear woman," the King responded, accompanying her to the door, "of course experiments are going along fine, and we're helping in any way we can, but this stuff about a bunny . . . And how could it have come across a secret plantation . . . What kind of nonsense is all this?"

Having just barely managed to see the widow out, the King dropped heavily into his armchair and said, staring dully into space:

"If only he could get up . . . That's all I need now . . ."

After that he summoned his secretary and gave him an order:

"If that witch tries one more time to get in to see me, grab her by the neck . . . but do it politely . . . Until further notice . . ."

"In respect to the neck or in respect to the politeness?" the secretary inquired, taking down the King's order in a businesslike way.

"In respect to the widow," the King replied, pondering the new difficulties he was now facing.

By the way, Ponderer's widow found herself in the same company some time later and she again met the rabbit who worked in the Royal Guards. She told him that he (such a responsible rabbit) had repeated such irresponsible nonsense about the King and the Queen then.

"I had to," the member of the Royal Guards replied, without even blinking.

The widow couldn't stop herself and hinted very obviously that she had had a conversation with the King himself on this very topic, and the King had personally ridiculed that rather sentimental myth.

"That means I had to do it then," the Royal Guards worker repeated firmly, and when he said this his ears stuck up straight and got firmer.

"Ah," everyone who was listening nodded with a feeling that they'd understood, they'd sensed the mystical sweetness in the firm significance of his words: Of course, what more is there to say . . .

And the First Widow of the kingdom nodded knowingly, although, as we have already had occasion to ascertain, she was in no way a shy rabbit.

As a matter of fact there was a law in the rabbits' kingdom, which not many of the rabbits understood, but which everyone had a good sense of. The law was: "If you swim in the King's direction, it is possible to go even faster than the royal speed."

And now everyone felt that the words of this rabbit who worked for the Royal Guards fit this law very well, and therefore it wasn't so terrible that the King had denied his story.

In the meantime, more and more odd things, each more surprising than the last, were turning up in the rabbits' kingdom. First of all, drunken rabbits had begun to appear; they roared out their stupid songs not only in the jungle, but also in the grounds around the royal palace. They had learned how to toss wild fruit into the hollows of trees, leave them there to ferment (having caulked up the hollow), and then they drank the alcoholic juice through a hole they'd made, after which they stopped up the hole with a dab of pitch. Sometimes they confused their holes with holes belonging to others, which caused a rash of foolish misunderstandings, not to mention the rabbits who walked around from hollow to hollow, and at times these hollows were guarded by real alcoholics, who gave full vent to their noble rage if they caught anyone sneaking some juice.

And quite a few drunken rabbits had begun to appear after they had made an amazing discovery — it turned out that the fermented elderberry juice, which until then had been known only in the form of ink in their kingdom, could also be a wonderful drink that made rabbits happy.

Actually, that discovery had been made long ago, but since the rabbits' society hadn't experienced any great need for it, word hadn't spread among them. The court Poet had in fact made the discovery. While he was composing his verses in a normal way, he once chewed off the upper tip of his flamingo feather quill, which he used for writing, and he accidentally sucked up several drops of elderberry juice through the tubular quill. After that he noticed that the elderberry juice was able to soothe his bitterness and that it somehow aided his creative thinking.

Finally, he had become convinced that his creative thinking needed some ink in it before it could take form as verses on his paper. It's possible that some secret record is being kept in there, he thought, and he stubbornly dipped his tubular pen in the inkwell, sucked the ink up, and at the same time paid attention to his inner being.

And that's how he lived, not really hiding his creative method, but not really advertising it either. Every morning his wife went off to the royal storehouse, where in addition to the other products, she received a bamboo pot full of ink. Since the supply of ink in the royal storehouse was endless, the treasurer usually didn't ask the Poet's wife why he was devouring so much ink. Or it's possible that he did ask, and it's possible that she even answered truthfully, but according to science, if there were no need in the rabbits' society for her answer at that time, then no one would have paid any attention to it.

At this time however, the rabbits were simply thirsting for her reply, and of course they heard it: "Well, what does your husband do, drink the ink?" the treasurer said without any malice, merely because he was surprised. Having taken the tap out of a barrel-shapped hollow container, he poured her a full pot. Then, having corked it, he offered it to her.

"He doesn't drink it. He sucks it up into his mouth," she replied.

"What do you mean he sucks it up?" the treasurer was surprised.

"Just that, he sucks it up through his pen," the wife replied.

"And nothing happens?" the treasurer was stunned.

"Nothing," the wife replied, "he works . . . only towards evening he does stammer a little."

"Does he stammer or does he stumble?" the treasurer asked.

"Both," the wife replied, "sometimes I have to . . ."

Several females, the wives of Rabbits Admitted to the Table, listened proudly to this conversation between the Poet's wife and the treasurer. As soon as she had left, the first of these women demanded a pot of ink, saying that her husband had sat down to spend many years writing the Glorious History of the Rabbit Kingdom! And so it went.

Then the widows, led by the First Widow of the kingdom, began to write memoirs about their deceased husbands, and they actually gathered in the evenings to sit, and as they called it, ink things up, recalling former days.

The ordinary rabbits, who heard about the properties

of the elderberry juice, dragged out a law that had long ago been forgotten— but which had never been repealed — it read: "Don't spare any ink for the education of the rabbits." This law had been put into effect by the King himself, when he had just begun to rule. Then he'd somehow gotten distracted and had given up on enlightenment, so the stores of ink had continued to expand. And now the rabbits were thirsting for Enlightenment.

Deciding to obtain at least some political advantage from these supplies, the King did not object. And within two months, when the supply of ink had been almost exhausted, the Chief Scholar, who had divided the quantity of ink squandered by the total number of rabbits in the kingdom, came to the joyful conclusion that the kingdom's populace now enjoyed universal literacy.

After that, the law about not sparing ink was repealed because of the triumphant victory of education, and new, smaller supplies of ink were carefully filtered for court use, by passing the elderberry juice through a thick layer of ferns.

The repeal of the law didn't upset the ordinary rabbits too much. They continued with their own self-education, fermenting ink from bunches of ripe elderberries.

Meanwhile, the mysterious bunny appeared here and there and always asked, with a kind of absentminded sadness, for cauliflower. Once the bunny even appeared on a branch of the carrot oak which grew under the palace windows.

"Unca King, me want cau'flower," it begged, swaying on the end of a branch right by the royal bedroom.

The Queen fainted in indignation, but the King managed to rouse the guards, who surrounded the oak tree, presuming that they could catch the bunny alive, or at the very least, dead. The bunny didn't give any verbal response, but from time to time it threw the totally inedible, but nonetheless rather heavy acorns down at the guards, with absentminded accuracy as well.

Some of the guards were severely wounded, but to make up for that the remaining ones grew even more furious. Bombarded by the falling acorn projectiles, they attacked and stormed the unlikely citadel, as the royal historians later described it.

The guards crawled up all the branches, but the bunny couldn't be found. Then they decided that it must have camouflaged itself in the tree's foliage, so they started to shake all the branches, stretching out a net made of savannah grass beneath each branch they shook.

Several more guards were wounded in these attempts, and finally a fairly heavy body fell into the net and was trapped there.

But alas, the King, who had come out to have a look at the rabbit who was disturbing the kingdom's peace, was even more depressed. Not only were thirty severely wounded guards carried past him as he was leaving the palace on his way to the oak tree, but to top it off, when he got to the net, and it was carefully untangled, all that turned up there was a squirrel.

"It's okay, we'll get down to the rabbit fur," the Chief of the Guards said and ordered the squirrel, together with the net, to be carefully taken into the room where rabbits accused of crimes were interrogated.

"One more attack like that, and I'll be left without an army," the King said bitterly, looking with disgust out over the field of battle.

As a matter of fact, the King's Guards were equivalent to the Royal Guards of the kingdom, and they were furthermore considered the army. The army was equipped with bamboo lances, bamboo sticks, and bamboo pipes, which they used to shoot cactus spines with. The destructive force of the flow gun was strong enough to down an average parrot, but it didn't have any effect on the skin of the natives, or, what's more, on the hide of a boa constrictor.

Essentially, the army's purpose was to chase off the

petty rodents who disputed over the rabbits' lands or burrows, and — this was its main task — to take action against rabbits who rebelled.

Having ordered that the branch which hung near the King's window be cut off — so that such incidents wouldn't be repeated — the King went into his palace to await the results of the interrogation.

In the meantime, it turned out to be impossible to interrogate the squirrel because of its stubborn silence. They weren't able to force it to talk because the squirrel's body, more precisely its ears, weren't adaptable to the single known method of torture then available in the kingdom.

That consisted of binding the rabbits' ears with a strong rope. The other end of the rope was thrown over a beam under the ceiling; they then pulled the rabbit up slightly, gave him this end of the rope to hold, and let him go. The large knot at the place in the rope where it had been tossed over the beam (they'd thought of everything, these clever tormentors!) didn't permit it to slip down on the side where the rabbit was hanging, ears bound up. In the end, in order to free himself from the pain of his ears being stretched, the hanging rabbit had to pull himself up with all his strength, in order finally to reach the beam.

If the rabbit subjected to these tortures, reached the beam and admitted his guilt, he was set free, after having paid the fine set for his crime. If he didn't confess, they lowered him again and repeated the torture.

The bunny who was thought to be disguised as a squirrel turned out to have such tiny ears that it was impossible to bind them with a rope. While they thought and tried to guess what they should do with this creature, news unexpectedly arrived from the jungle: the bunny had escaped and had already begged some cauliflower from several responsible rabbits.

The Chief of the Guards, who felt very ashamed, was forced to let the squirrel go. However, the rabbit snipers were given a secret order: that if the squirrel didn't jump up into the nearest tree it chanced upon after it was freed, but ran past, it should be shot for attempting to escape. Fortunately for itself, the squirrel jumped up into the first tree it found.

Meanwhile, the rabbits' disobedience increased with each passing day. The morning prognosis about the effect of the hypnosis was met with brazen hooting when announced by a herald at the Royal Meadow.

And a scandalous story almost created a rift in the friendly relations between the rabbits and the monkeys. In fact, one of Ponderer's sons (there were four of them, by the way, all regular bullies) had caught the young marmoset by a watering hole and had beaten her up. He gave as his reason the fact that she had known then that his father was being betrayed, but she hadn't told anyone about it. The marmoset's mother demanded that this unrestrained rabbit be punished, because he had demanded from her daughter what should have by rights been demanded of other rabbits. The most delicate diplomacy was put into effect to squelch the scandal, because it touched on the interests of persons too highly placed.

And the ill-intentioned bunny continued to appear here and there. The Royal Guard ran itself into the ground looking in all the corners of the kingdom. The fact was that each new appearance by the bunny, with its mocking request, made the grandiose program for raising cauliflower a little more ridiculous.

The bunny's distinctive features were written down on a cabbage leaf with the purpose of attracting the rabbits' attention; these leaves then were hung on many trees in the jungle. They had, however, been placed rather high, so that the rabbits could read the royal edict, but not eat it.

Nonetheless, the ill-intentioned bunny disappeared without a trace each time.

"It's a conspiracy," the Chief of the Royal Guards said,

"a conspiracy which has deep roots in those admitted to the table."

A drunken rabbit was seized once because it had been tailed from the Royal Meadow to its burrow, and its rambling but suspicious muttering had been heard and written down.

". . . And he was saying to me, "the sot said, "I'll give you some cauliflower, cauliflower . . . And I say to him: What do I need your old cauliflower for? I saw it in a grave, your cauliflower. I, for instance, have drunk my elderberry wine, I've tasted carrots which I myself dug up from a native's garden . . . But who's seen your cauliflower? And he says to me: I give you cauliflower, I give you everything, but you're ungrateful . . . And I say to him — You give us everything? No, you give us nuthin', we give you nuthin'. But then he says again: I give you cauliflower, everything . . ."

The rabbit was seized and sent to the Chief of the Guards. In many ways he seemed to resemble the rabbit who had crossed the King's path on that famous stroll, who had disappeared into the savannah with his spiteful muttering. It was difficult to get anything out of him that evening, but in the morning he was sent again to the Chief for interrogation.

The Chief of the Royal Guards was sitting in his study, preparing for the interrogation, sharpening his pens, looking at the drunkard who had muttered those suspicious words the evening before.

More precisely, he didn't exactly look at him, rather at his ears. Over these many years of duty, he had become accustomed to judging rabbits under investigation by the shape of their ears. Certain ears, which were narrow at the base, broadened rather abruptly (to the trained eye, of course), and this gave the Chief of the Guards true aesthetic pleasure. During the hanging such ears would never slip out of the loop, even if they were tied in a bow.

And this conspirator had just that kind of ears. The Chief of the Guards was already certain that he was indeed a conspirator. Even his ears served (in an indirect way, it's true) as circumstantial evidence of his guilt.

The drunken criminal, who clearly didn't have a clue about the suggestive shape of his ears, never took his eyes off the inkwell, which was no less tempting because the secretary had just then filled it with fresh elderberry juice, right before his eyes.

"So, are we going to play at being silent?" the Chief finally said and moved the inkwell slightly closer to himself. The criminal standing near the desk, involuntarily moved a little in the direction of the inkwell.

"Unca Chief, me want cau'flower." He suddenly heard that familiar voice.

The Chief of the Guards shuddered, raised his head, and saw the bunny sitting on his window sill; its sad expression seemed to imply it was listening for something it never heard, looking for something it never saw.

The Chief of the Guards shifted his gaze to the drunk to ascertain any connection between him and the bunny's appearance. But the drunkard was obviously totally preoccupied with feasting his eyes on the inkwell, which had been filled with fresh ink, and it seemed he hadn't heard anything at all.

"Look at the window," the Chief said softly and nodded at the besotted rabbit. He decided that the unexpected sight of the bunny would confuse him, if they were indeed related.

"Son?" the drunk asked, squinting at the window, apparently not able to tear himself away from the inkwell at all. No, it was clear that he didn't know it, the Chief thought.

"If I had a son like that, I'd . . ." he mumbled, and he fell silent, fixing his gaze on the sad bunny. The thing was that the window, which was covered by mica, had been closed. So where had it come from? It just didn't make any sense.

"Do you know with whom you're speaking?" the Chief of the Guards asked, feverishly trying to figure out how the bunny's appearance would be reflected in the inner life of the palace, and in what way he could connect its appearance to the conspiracy of those Admitted to the Table.

"I know," the bunny suddenly confirmed, and this time its sad voice seemed to hint that it couldn't expect anything good to come from its knowledge.

"That means you've come to spill the beans," the Chief said, expressing his joy at having figured out the riddle. Up to that time, the bunny had never said anything except its mocking little sentence.

But now, having turned up in his office, it had begun to speak. The Chief of the Guards felt that something grand was in the offering. He hummed and rubbed his paws together with pleasure. His mind was working with unusual vigor.

"I know how you turned up in the palace," the Chief said. "While we were storming the oak tree, you hopped into the King's bedroom. That's why we didn't find you then . . . But how did you get to the Guards' section? And keep in mind that a voluntary confession will make things easier for you."

"I have a pass," the bunny said sadly, and adding, as if to hint about his eternal orphanhood, "for one person."

"Well, okay, a pass," the Chief of the Guards agreed, quietly rejoicing inside. "But who gave it to you? I know, of course, but I'd rather you told me yourself . . ."

"You did," the bunny said sadly and showed him something in its paw.

"I did?!" the Chief of the Guards asked him again, choking with rage and guessing simultaneously that the conspirators were conducting their intrigue against him in this insidious way.

"Yes, you," the bunny repeated sadly, and with unprecedented insolence it offered him some sort of bedraggled scrap of cabbage leaf, which didn't resemble a pass at all, even from a distance.

This insolence caused the Chief of the Royal Guards to explode prematurely. He grabbed a heavy coconut (an ancient gift from a delegation of marmosets) and hurled it at the bunny.

The heavy coconut broke through the mica window and several seconds later crashed onto the inner courtyard of the royal palace. It was evident from the sound that it had broken open and the liquid had splashed out of it.

"It broke," the bunny said with mocking ambiguity, or so it seemed to the Chief of the Guards.

Without saying another word, the bunny turned toward the window, bent its ears down with its paw (lest they be cut), went out to the other side, and disappeared behind the window ledge. For a few more seconds, its ears still stuck up near the window, and it was clearly hanging from the ledge, trying to decide where to jump.

As soon as the ears had disappeared, the Chief of the Guards jumped up from his desk, went over to the window sill, and carefully putting his head through the hole, he shouted down:

"Has anyone passed by?"

The guards were walking below, picking up pieces of the coconut, and carefully licking them. It looked like a pot of money had fallen from some high place and broken there, and that they were searching for the money that had fallen out. One of them, who'd gotten a solid chunk of the coconut, held it over his upturned face (because he had been the first to notice the Chief), and carefully letting the last drops fall into his mouth, replied:

"No one, Chief!"

The other guards also raised their heads and suddenly began shouting:

"Thank you, Chief! Throw down another one!"

The Chief didn't say anything and pulled his head back through the broken window. Then he noticed on the window sill a very faded piece of cabbage leaf with the seal of the royal storehouse.

"The devil alone knows what's going on," the Chief said, throwing the cabbage leaf away and sitting down.

"Did the bunny split?" the drunk asked, coming to life and looking at where the cabbage leaf had fallen.

The Chief looked at him. Their eyes met.

"Yeah, split," the drunk answered himself, and his eyes shone with the guilty brilliance of blackmail. "That's not good . . . And what's more, it'd come to give itself up, and you chucked it out by heaving a state-property coconut at it."

"Okay, you can go home now," the Chief said sternly. "And keep this in mind: You didn't hear anything, you didn't see anything."

"I'm goin', I'm goin'," the drunk said, not budging at all, his eyes once again fixed on the inkwell. "But really, if someone came to surrender, and what's more, a royal criminal . . . It's not allowed to frighten it by heaving a state-property coconut . . ."

"Okay, have a drink and then go," the Chief of the Guards said and nodded at the inkwell.

"To your health, Chief," the rabbit said and emptied the rather capacious inkwell in one gulp. At the same time, he bent over and picked up the cabbage leaf, which the Chief had thrown on the floor. He shook it, wiped it a couple of times on his chest, sniffed it, and popped it in his mouth. He began to chew, at the same time trying to show that he had picked up something useless from the floor and put it in his mouth, otherwise, he would have put it on the desk.

Let him swallow it, it's better that way, the Chief thought absentmindedly, noting in passing how quickly the ordinary rabbits became so impudent.

"It's one from the Queen, it's clean," the drunk final-
ly exhaled, "that's something else . . ."

Having gotten quickly plastered, he began to instruct
the Chief of the Guards in how to best capture the outlaw
bunny, at the same time continuing to hold the inkwell in
his paw, hinting with the expression of an extortionist.

But then the Chief of the Guards looked at him with
his famous glance, which quickly brought the drunk to his
senses.

"Everything's clear, Chief," the drunkard said, putting
the inkwell on the desk and moving backwards. Finally, he
left the room.

That's it, the Chief thought, satisfied by the effect of
his look. He wondered if the bunny mightn't be part of some
conspiracy in the court, and even if it's not connected yet,
wouldn't it be right to connect its appearance with the still
undiscovered conspiracy among those Admitted to the
Table?

He called his secretary and asked him if anyone had
called on him this morning.

"There was one bunny that came," the secretary re-
plied, "Said you were looking for it."

"Well, what did you do?" the Chief asked.

"Well, I told it," the secretary responded, "if the Chief
of the Guards needs you, go in and wait. What happened?"

"That means no matter who asks for me," the Chief
of the Guards said, "you tell him to go in and wait!"

"But it did have a royal cabbage leaf," the secretary re-
plied, "it was an old one, but it was still a valid pass. But
what's this? A broken window, and your ear's all bloody!
An attempt on your life!!!"

"Fortunately for the kingdom, it was unsuccessful," the
Chief of the Guards said. "But what a viper! It said that
I'd given it the pass, meaning the cabbage leaf, on the
Queen's orders. It's good that there were witnesses. There's
a dangerous criminal in the palace! Close all the entrances

and especially the exits! Pour me some fresh ink, but not in the inkwell, in a goblet, dammit! I think the criminal's hiding among the royal ballerinas. We'll have to check them out very, very carefully!"

Despite the fact that all the entrances and especially all the exits of the royal palace had been sealed off, the next day the King received most unpleasant news: the bunny had made another sortie on the outskirts of the kingdom.

The Chief Treasurer had told of this in a secret denunciation. The fact is that in connection with these various alarms, the King had given orders to set up a secret supply of cabbage in the most remote corner of his kingdom. If the kingdom did indeed fall, he'd thought he could take his wife and closest associates there, color their skin with black elderberry juice, and live as a wealthy family of Negro rabbits, who had come from a distant land.

And so when the Chief Treasurer had been taking some more cabbages to the storehouse the day before, accompanied by five workers, they had noticed the bunny, sitting at the top of the pyramid of stacked cabbages, like a little figure from a fairy tale — Koshchey the Deathless, who used to sit on a pile of natives' skull, which were, by the way, absolutely inedible, unlike cabbages.

Having seen the rabbits, it as usual asked for cauliflower, which sounded particularly mocking, seeing that it was sitting on a whole mountain of ordinary cabbage. It sounded as if it were convinced of the total alimentary unsuitability of the supplies on which it was sitting.

"Did it say anything about me?" the King asked, having heard the story in a gloomy frame of mind.

"No," the Treasurer replied. "No, but it's interesting that when one of the workers climbed to the top, it turned out that instead of finding a bunny there, he found a head of cabbage with two torn leaves, which from the bottom resembled a bunny."

"It's very clear," the King responded gloomily, "the

secret storehouse has been discovered . . . And that ninny,
the Chief of the Guards, is looking for the bunny at the
palace, and he's still feeling up my ballerinas. I have to say,
dear friends, that in two or three months the kingdom will
disintegrate as the result of a decrease in the boas' produc-
tive energy.''

12

But no, the rabbits' kingdom didn't collapse. Because pre-
cisely on that historic day the Hermit Boa came back (that's
why it's historic) to the underground palace of the Great
Python and told of his discovery.

The Great Python ordered the whole nation of boas,
which had been considerably thinned out, to gather. Some
of them had to be dragged there, they were so weak from
starvation.

One boa, who had climbed up onto the fig tree that grew
by the entrance to the Great Python's palace, fell from his
branch during the singing of the anthem and crashed down
right next to the Tsar. The Tsar, who had been forced to
break off the anthem, waited to see what he would do next.

The boa, embarrassed by the shameful fall and the in-
delicate proximity of this accident to the spot where the
Great Python was lying, tried to slink away, jerking his dis-
obedient body with no effect, however, which produced
an especially oppressive impression on the Tsar and those
lying near him.

''Well, just lie there, for the Great Dragon's sake,'' the
Tsar finally said, having already decided not to resume sing-
ing the anthem. He then told everyone, in summary form,
especially those boas who would have been too young,
about how the Hermit had been punished in his time, and

now he had returned with an interesting proposal.

With modest dignity, the now forgiven Hermit spoke about his theoretical discovery and his experimental test, which had been completely successful. The boas, who had been listening unhappily to the Hermit's tale, began to ask questions.

"But perhaps this was a half-dead rabbit?" asked the boa who was accustomed to seeing everything in a gloomy light. "Perhaps it wasn't even worth smothering?"

"Of course," the Hermit replied, "the rabbit wasn't in the best of shape. But keep in mind that I had been feeding on lizards and mice in that damned desert, I was barely able to move."

"Well, why are you saying all this about yourself?" the boas hissed in response. "Look at us, look at what we've become."

"I know," the Hermit replied with even more noticeable modest dignity "that's why I've returned . . . Now I feel calm and confident, having been able to capture a rabbit with a totally new method without using hypnosis."

"When did you digest it?" the Great Python suddenly asked.

"Today," the Hermit replied. "Didn't I tell you?"

"That's fine for you," the Great Python sighed, "you've had breakfast, but I still haven't had anything to eat."

The boas sensed something, though they didn't know quite what. Perhaps that the Great Python had complained in vain, but, more likely, that he was jealous of the Hermit. He was jealous — that meant he had recognized the boa's superiority. At that moment the spirit of doubt, doubt about the Great Python, floated over the boas. It's true, as with the rabbits, relations within the tribe had been shaken terribly, and again this morning a hunter had permitted himself a daring outburst.

"Listen, just how old is our Great Python?" one of the boas in the back rows asked another.

"Who knows?" he hissed, "it's better to listen to the Hermit, he's talking business . . ."

The questions continued to fly. The Hermit answered all of them with ever increasing precision and dignity.

"What are the upper and lower limits of suffocation?"

"My brother boas," the Hermit replied, "I still can't say anything about the upper and lower limits, but I can say with certainty that we can deal with a rabbit by using the golden mean."

"That's the main thing," the boas hissed contentedly.

"Oh, the charming and insidious golden mean," signed one boa, the one who'd been beaten by the natives for trying to get the head of cabbage for the female rabbit.

"I don't know about the lower limit," the Great Python said and looked rather strangely at the boas, "but we'll find out about the upper limit right now . . . Smother Stubby!"

The boas shuddered in surprise. The Hermit threw himself at Stubby, but although he was lying on the ground this time, still he was close to a tree, and he managed to turn over and shinny up a palm tree.

"Smother him on the tree!" the Great Python shouted, getting excited.

"But I don't know how to smother in trees!" the Hermit replied.

"You gonna wait till he slithers down?" one of the boas asked drearily.

"Well, I'm never gonna come down," Stubby replied. "There's enough food here."

The boas started to insult Stubby, but he didn't pay any attention to their hissing. He stretched over to a bunch of bananas on a neighboring tree and began to eat them, tossing the skins down onto the boas' backs, which made them quiver nervously.

"You're a monkey, not a boa constrictor," the Great Python said and again looked out over his nation. "Then we'll try Squinter . . . Where's Squinter?"

"Your wish is my command," the Hermit said, just as modestly and precisely.

"Why not?" Squinter said. "I'm too old to change my ways now . . . You can smother me . . ."

The Hermit coiled and threw himself at Squinter. They intertwined, but Squinter hung listlessly from the Hermit, just as a tired boxer in our times hangs onto his opponent.

"Put up a fight, resist!" the Tsar shouted, "we need more experience with jungle conditions."

"What kind of resistance?" Squinter sighed and gave up the ghost.

"Although he died for the good of the cause," the Great Python said, "I have always maintained that a boa who lets a rabbit talk inside him is not the kind of boa we need."

"It's characteristic," the Hermit noted, freeing himself from Squinter's dead body, "that the experiment goes better if the creature being studied trembles, if it puts up some resistance. This thrashing around arouses the muscle system and brings it into action."

"Drag him away somewhere," the Great Python said. "We're entering a new era, and there won't be any invalids like Squinter or degenerates like Stubby, who we will still shake down from this tree. I will name the Hermit as my first vice president and pretender to the crown of the Great Python (that's me), during his lifetime. Spread out into the jungles! Train, develop your nature!"

With these words, he departed for his underground palace, having taken along his successor for a personal chat.

And from that day on the boas began to train strenuously under the Hermit's guidance. He had worked out a series of classical exercises for developing the smothering muscles.

Thus, for example, two groups of boas were invovled in a tug of war, using an outstretched boa instead of a rope. A stuffed rabbit was placed on the sandy bank of a river, where they worked on leaping.

Another exercise enjoyed particular success. A boa chose two youngish trees which were growing close to each other; he crawled to the top of one and fastened his tail section around it. Then he lunged at the top of the other tree; having gripped it with his front section, he tensed and relaxed his body, tensed and relaxed. He could train like this for hours, taking care that the tops of the trees bent at the same angle of inclination, which served to develop the whole muscle system equally.

One fine day, the Hermit gathered the boas and announced to them that the Great Python had died, but that his body would be eternally on display beside his hunting trophies, since the sculptor was going to make him into a mummy.

"In accordance with the Great Python's wish," he said finally, not losing his dignity, and at the same time sharpening his accuracy, "a boa will rule over the boas, that means, I will. From now on there will be no more palaces . . . The Great Python's palace will now be known as the Hermit's Cell.

"May I ask a question?" one of the boas hissed.

"Yes," the Hermit nodded.

"Is it possible to address you as the Great Hermit, in honor of all your deeds?"

"Personally speaking, I don't need that, but if you like, you may," the Great Hermit replied, just as modestly and accurately.

Meanwhile, the boas continued with their training, combining it with experiments on live rabbits. At first many of the boas weren't very accurate in their work, but gradually they became more and more accomplished at methods of suffocation. The first time a boa leaped toward a rabbit, for example, he often missed; he landed with a splat next to the prey, after which the rabbit took off, and the boa crawled into the bushes with a smashed-up stomach.

Several boas had gotten themselves so twisted up in

the process of coiling and smothering that they had to spend a lot of time afterward untying themselves. And one boa got so tangled up in knots (it's true that he was strangling a rather large monkey), that he never did get untangled.

They brought him in a rather sad state to the palace, that is, to the Hermit's Cell, where the doctors looked him over and recommended amputating part of the body, in order to save his life.

"That's not very profitable," the Great Hermit rejected the suggestion. "Drown him in the river . . . We had an invalid once . . ."

The guards dragged the unlucky wretch to the river and drowned him. In a few days the Great Hermit gave a sermon on the topic "Smothering Is Not an End in Itself." After that a number of classic loop knots were worked out, and the cases of boas being tangled in their own knots significantly decreased.

Interesting changes took place in the exhibition of the Great Python's trophies. A number of them were given to boas so they could work on their leaps and squeezing. Of course the most valuable exhibits, including above all the Native in His Prime, were kept.

Instead of the former pieces, the collection had been enlarged, starting with the display of a stuffed rabbit who was the first to be dealt with in the new way. And a number of old trophies had been restored according to the Great Hermit's recollections. The Great Hermit's personal trophies concluded with the mummy of the Great Python with his eyes open, which created an awesome ambiguity and hinted rather frighteningly that the Python had been the Great Hermit's most brilliant kill. And what's more, there had been dark rumors among the boas that not long before the Great Python's death, he had either been deprived of the right to have a say, or deprived of the gift of speech.

It's time, however, to return to our rabbits.

At first none of them were upset by the news about the

boas' new behavior. Those rabbits which the boas had managed to suffocate, quite naturally, couldn't say anything about this to their fellow rabbits. And those who were spared, because the boas slammed to the ground near them, clumsily and heavily, couldn't understand this at all.

The rabbits began to laugh at these incidents and even thought for the longest time that the boas were throwing themselves down from trees in an attempt to stun them with their own weight, since the hypnosis was no longer working.

Then rumors started filtering in to the King that not far from the green hill where the eternal flame that honored Ponderer was lit each Sunday, the boas had erected a monument to the Unknown Rabbit, to whom they paid homage each day, throwing themselves at it and trying to embrace it.

"They're totally nuts," the King said when he heard that.

"Now, instead of the Great Python, they have some kind of Hermit," the Chief of the Guards said.

"Actually, they're praying," the Wise Old Rabbit announced his solution.

"Praying?!" the King smiled bitterly. "And how did you figure out this was a sign of prayer?"

But the Wise Old Rabbit hadn't had time to think of an answer because the King's secretary strode into his office and whispered something in his ear.

"Bring her in," the King said, noticeably more alert.

A moment later a mauled female rabbit hobbled into the King's study.

"Tell us your story," the King said.

And this is what the female rabbit told. It seems she had been grazing on the edge of the jungle, where it bordered on the savannah, when a boa unexpectedly attacked her. It gripped her in its coils and began to smother her. She freed herself from its embrace with great difficulty and managed to escape.

"It didn't try to hypnotize you?" the King inquired.

"What do you mean hypnotize?" the rabbit replied. "I've never felt such pain in my entire life . . . Look, it dislocated my paw . . ."

"Perhaps it was attempted rape?" the Chief Scholar suggested.

"Very interesting!" the Queen exclaimed.

"Let one of them dislocate your paw," the rabbit said boldly, "and see how interesting it'll be . . ."

"Who do you think you're speaking to?" the Chief of the Guards cut her off menacingly.

"Quiet, quiet," the King said, paying no attention to the rabbit's disrespectul tone. "But still, could you feel what it was the boa wanted from you?"

"I felt that he wanted to suffocate me," the rabbit replied, and by the expression on her face it was clear she was trying very hard to turn up her dim powers of imagination.

"Well, what for," the King asked impatiently.

"I don't know what for," she replied.

"Okay dearie, you can go now," the King said, patting her on the shoulder and adding to the secretary: "Take care of her, see that she gets assistance every week, the same as someone wounded in the service of the state would get."

When the rabbit had thanked the King and gone out with the secretary, the King turned to his aides:

"Well, what do you say to this?"

"I'd say, dear, that you've really let your subjects get out of hand," the Queen said.

"You should tighten up," the Chief of the Guards concurred.

The others remained silent.

"In my opinion, this is a very interesting case," the King was a bit more alert. "Everything is falling into place now . . . an increasing number of rabbits are disappearing without a trace . . . the female rabbit who was roughed up

. . . the boa's strange exercises . . . They've worked out a new weapon — smothering!''

''Sire, you're a genius!'' the Wise Old Rabbit exclaimed. ''Why do you need me, the scientists and scholars? Why do you need the Chief of the Guards, when you are everything?''

''Calm down,'' the King replied, ''I only made the necessary connections. We have to alert the rabbits to this terrible danger which threatens them . . . Who said it wasn't necessary to develop one's nature? I did. Now they've reached the point where they're breaking the bones of living rabbits. Multiply, and do it ahead of schedule — that will be our weapon against the boas!''

The news about the boas' terrible new weapon, which demanded the rabbits' unity as never before, was unfortunately confirmed very soon and in the most tragic way. The rabbits threw the stuffed rabbit into the river, the ones the boas had been training on, but it was already too late. Their attempts to chew through the young tree, so that the boas couldn't work on their smothering muscles, also showed poor results. The boas started to lie in wait for rabbits near young trees which grew in pairs. And really, was it possible to chew through all the young trees that grew in pairs?

Yearner's activities had less and less success among the rabbits after the boas had begun to smother them without using hypnosis.

The Chief of the Guards offered from time to time to hang him up by his ears, but the King rejected this extreme measure, feeling that while the boas were displaying true firmness in regard to the rabbits, he had to be kinder with them, otherwise, they'd lose all hope.

Generally, the King regained his sense of humor, that rather coarse brand of humor his people understood and valued so highly.

''It seems that someone once promised us he'd run

alongside a boa," the King used to say at rabbits' meetings, which invariably brought out the rabbits' friendly laughter. Usually the joke was based on Yearner's proposal to institute reforms of one kind or another.

"But you have to understand that circumstances are completely different now," Yearner said in response to all these unpleasant reminders.

"That's right," the King nodded, "try to develop your nature and it'll end up with the boas flying to catch rabbits. That's what my father told me in those distant years when no one could even imagine that the boas would turn their backs on hypnosis."

The rabbits again quieted down and obeyed the law more. Now they regularly brought their garden tax to the royal storehouse. And though they didn't exactly start drinking less, they did drink at home in their burrows, not just anywhere. Yearner, recalling his Teacher's saying about wisdom, that if it couldn't do good, then it should at least try to lengthen evil's path, tried to obtain an improvement in the rabbits' safety from the Chief Scholar and his whole chancellery.

Since the time when the boas had started pouncing on rabbits (mostly out of frustation at first), the Chief Scholar had stopped coming out of the palace. Actually, he came out only during meetings, and of course never went farther than the Royal Meadow. There couldn't even be any discussion of his conducting his scientific experiments under field conditions.

It's true that after a long time spent working, which had in fact included questioning those rabbits who had managed to escape, he had come up with the insightful formula that the length of a boa's jump is equal to the square of its own length.

Although struck by the crisp attractiveness of the formula, the rabbits still complained, under Yearner's influence, that it wasn't possible to apply this formula in practice. The King, who admitted in part that their complaints were valid, tried to console them.

"You have in your hands the correct theory," the King said, "and that's better than nothing."

"The theory may be correct," the rabbits replied, "but how can it be used, when we don't know the length of the boas attacking us.

"That's also true," the King agreed, and finding Yearner with his eyes, he added: "By the way, someone here promised to run alongside a boa . . . Perhaps he could measure five or six boas, and then we could arrive at the average length of an attacking boa . . ."

"But you know that times are different now," Yearner replied, lowering his head in shame.

"I not only know it now, I knew it then," the King invariably responded, which always brought the rabbits to a state of quiet ecstasy.

"He knew it then," the rabbits repeated, dispersing and going to their burrows after the meeting. "Our King's really a bright guy."

Despite their misfortunes, more likely thanks to these calamities, the rabbits continued to multiply ahead of schedule, and again thanks to their misfortunes, these mortals continued to steal from the natives' gardens with even greater diligence, together with their confederates in this matter, the monkeys.

Finally the natives, who had developed their natural tendency to love their gardens, managed to make an agreement with the Great Hermit to allow boas to be on duty at the gardens as living traps. It was rather easy to agree on the proper payment.

"Whatever you can catch, you can eat," the natives offered. The boas willingly carried out their duties, because when the rabbits and monkeys came to the gardens and stuffed themselves with fruits and vegetables, they became quite careless.

"If only I'd known then that these bastards would be guarding the corn too," the same marmoset said with elegaic sadness, as she picked lice out of her granddaughter's hair, who had never heard anything about Sharpie, let alone about Ponderer, the one who was betrayed.

By the way, once when a boa had been assigned to duty at a cornfield, he returned rather embarrassed, which was noticed by some of the other boas.

"What happened?" they asked him.

"It seems I made a mistake," he replied, lying down in a cool ravine not far from the Great Hermit's Cell. "Instead of swallowing a marmoset, I got the master's wife."

"Well, how was she?" the boas, who were resting in the ravine, asked.

"Okay, nothing special," the boa replied. "I wonder if that native will complain to the Great Hermit."

"Who knows," said an elderly boa, who still looked sort of young. "Sometimes they don't . . . It happens that one of our brothers will be tempted by a nice, plump native woman — and nothing happens. But if you swallow one of the little ones, then the whole jungle hears about it . . ."

"Well, this one was thin and stringy . . . At first I took her for a monkey in the dark, but later I thought . . . I'll have to answer for this."

"You did right," the elderly boa said, "it's better not to leave the corpse there . . . Because the natives have a lot to drink every now and again, just like the rabbits, and they forget about everything that happened. A guy'll wake up and not be able to remember whether he gave his wife to someone as a gift, or he simply chased her away . . ."

"By the way," the elderly boa added, because he liked to help the younger, inexperienced boas, though he did it in a rather fussy way: "Before you finish digesting her, leave your shit at the treasure room. The natives are easily calmed down if there's some little bit of iron left behind as a souvenir of the person who was swallowed . . ."

That elderly boa seemed to be clairvoyant. Two weeks later, rumors reached the husband that his wife had been swallowed by the very boa assigned to stand watch over his garden. And what was especially insulting was that the boa had gleefully told several other boas that he'd mistaken her for a monkey.

And so he came to the Great Hermit to complain. Before he received the native, he ordered the curtains to be drawn in front of the Native in His Prime, out of respect for the ancient tradition.

"Your boa's done swallowed my wife," he began to complain to the Great Hermit, stressing particularly the insulting comparison with a monkey.

"We'll punish him" the Great Hermit replied. "By the way, why don't you go to our treasure room and take back whatever decorations she was wearing."

"Thanks, master," the native bowed to him, "My other wife'll take 'em."

"Well, he's reconciled," the Great Hermit said, "I've always insisted on maintaining friendly relations with the natives . . ."

Despite this unpleasant incident, the native was pleased with the way he had been received and asked if in the future his field could always have a boa on duty. It's true that, at the end, their conversation developed a certain awkwardness. Looking over the stuffed exhibits and being justifiably ecstatic about the sculptor boa's art, the native pointed to the mummy of the Great Python and said:

"He looks jes' like real . . ."

"But he is real," the Great Hermit replied, "only disemboweled and filled with pitch."

"An' are they doin' one of y'all there?" the stupid native nodded at the concealed exhibit of the Native in His Prime.

"More like they're making one of you," the Great Hermit replied in a vague, rather terrifying way, and the native hurried out. The Hermit didn't like to talk about his own death. He didn't even like to talk about others' deaths, if that other creature's death would remind him of his own.

In short, after the Hermit's ascension to the throne, the rabbits' and boas' life entered a new, though already smooth and deep rut: the rabbits robbed for their pleasure, and the boas smothered for theirs.

"Multiply ahead of schedule and wait for the Cauliflower," the King used to say, "that's the source of our historic optimism."

And the rabbits continued to multiply successfully, impatiently expecting the cauliflower.

"You're alive, I'm alive," the female rabbits used to say to their husbands in the evenings, "our kids are alive, that means the King must be right . . ."

The rabbits, however, didn't understand that only the rabbits who were living were able to take part in this roll call.

"If only the Teacher were alive," Yearner sighed. "What can I do alone now, under these new circumstances?"

Still, in accordance with Ponderer's saying, he tried to develop the rabbits' ability to flee quickly, in order to lengthen evil's path.

Ponderer's widow organized a volunteer society of young admirers of the cauliflower. On Sundays, when they solemnly lit the eternal flame over Ponderer's symbolic grave on the green hill, she gathered together the members of the society and recalled her unforgettable husband's endless and varied utterances about that remarkable product of the future. The vividness of her recollections about cauliflower was maintained by a firm head of ordinary cabbage from the royal supplies.

Once, when the King and Queen had grown quite old, they were sunning themselves in the evening, standing by a window, the same one into which the bunny had looked from the carrot oak and begged for cauliflower.

"Sharpie, was he the one with the pretty eyes, or was

he the one who betrayed the Teacher?" the Queen suddenly asked the King. By the way, the court cosmeticians had rather bravely given the Queen's face the features of her former beauty, though few actually remembered what she had looked like in her youth.

"I don't really . . . It's seems they were related," the King replied, picking his teeth with an eagle feather. "But do you know who I'm sick and tired of? Ponderer's widow."

The King's last remark, although not at all related to the Queen's question, was still understandable. She really had kept it up too long. Some of her own children and granchildren had already perished by then, but she was still telling stories from Ponderer's life, always recalling new details from their heart-to-heart talks about cauliflower.

But it was also possible to understand her; she would have missed her free royal cabbage, which gave her the strength to live so long. In short, it's possible to understand everyone if there's enough time and the will to do it.

It's interesting that several of the aged rabbits very much idealized their former lives, during the period of hypnosis, when they were talking with the younger rabbits.

"It used to be," they said, "that you were out strolling in the jungle, and you'd meet Squinter, but you could pass by without even stopping, if you kept to his safe side. Or you'd meet Stubby, he'd look at you and not even want to . . . Why? Because he used to stuff himself with bananas, just like a monkey."

"But where are they now?" the younger rabbits asked, envying such a free life.

"The boas smothered Squinter," one of the old rabbits replied, "and Stubby degenerated into another animal and took a different name."

"You were lucky," the young rabbits sighed.

"Before, no one would have believed," the old rabbits were incensed, "that the natives would use boas against rabbits . . ."

"And what about drinking? They used to give away pure elderberry juice for free," the aged alcoholics recalled. "If you wanted, you could learn to write, and if you wanted to drink it, it was your own business."

"But you're forgetting the main thing," one reminded them, "under hypnosis, if you were already destined to die, they put you in a trance so you couldn't feel anything."

"And now the ordinary rabbits drink rotgut," one aged alcoholic didn't want to change the subject, "the elderberry juice only goes to the Admittees . . ."

"In short," one of the oldest rabbits sighed, "it was a well-ordered life."

It's amazing that when the elderly boa constrictors shared their reminiscences with the younger ones, they also said things had been better before. And by doing this, they as usual exaggerated quite a bit too.

"The way it was under hypnosis," one of the ancient boas related, "you're creeping in the jungle, and you meet a rabbit. Zap, and it stops in its tracks! You meet another one — again you stop it in its tracks! A female boa slithers along and cleans up after you. And what kind of rabbits were they? The ones nowadays are like rats compared to those ones. You swallowed one then and you didn't need any digestive juices — it just digested itself in peace. And now you have to suffocate it, it squeals and tries to get away, to show you something. What is there to show . . .?"

"Oh, boas really lived then," the younger boas sighed dreamily.

"It was a well-ordered life," an old boa concluded, and added, after some reflection, as if fearing some wrong interpretation: "under hypnosis."

"They think it's easy to smother your prey," one of the old boas used to say, lying down to sleep and coiling his gout-filled body with difficulty. Although to look at him you wouldn't guess at all that he was the same boa we knew, the one accustomed to seeing everything in a gloomy light, in fact it really was him.

13

And that's all I've heard about the rather sad history of relations between rabbits and boa constrictors. If someone knows any interesting details that I've omitted, I'd be happy to receive them. It's best to send a letter, okay to telephone, and even better to keep them to yourself — I'm sick of this topic.

I had some scientific doubts when I was writing all this down. I didn't know, for example, if boa constrictors had actually hypnotized rabbits, or if it had just seemed that way from the sidelines.

For some reason, there's nothing about it in Brehm's *Life of the Animals.* All my acquaintances tend to believe that the boas did indeed hypnotize rabbits, though no one could fully confirm this.

And among my friends there isn't one real authority on snakes. I recalled that one of my half-forgotten acquaintances liked to say, when going on a business trip to the Kara-Kum desert: "I'm going to the snakes . . ."

Although I knew that he was a geologist by profession, I thought that he might have been studying snakes on the side. After some difficulty I found his telephone number and tried very long and unsuccessfully to remind him about this expression, but for some reason he denied everything, stressing that he might have been dissatisfied with one or two of his co-workers at the branch of their Central Asian Institute, but he couldn't recall feeling that way about the whole collective.

Finally he asked me who I was and why I was interested in such things, although I had indeed begun with precisely this information. He had apparently not been listening very attentively when I was speaking, and due to my Eastern name, he had taken me for one of his co-workers.

"Oh, it's you, old buddy," he said, quite happy that

he'd finally grasped who I was, "I thought you were one of my anonymous contacts . . . No, there weren't any snakes there, didn't see hide nor hair . . . Although, honestly speaking some real snakes . . ."

Since I wasn't interested in snakes in the figurative sense, I stopped listening to his carping and moaning, and I hung up at the first opportunity.

"You know, they showed that on TV," one woman said, after I'd started to talk about boa constrictors at one gathering.

"And you saw it yourself?" I asked, my hopes raised.

"Of course," she said, turning away from the mirror where she'd been observing herself with the same pedagogical severity all women use when looking at themselves in the mirror. They seem to reproach their own looks, not so much for being good, but rather for their potential to be much better.

"Well, what happened?" I asked, trembling with curiosity.

"I turned away," she said and looked at me even more significantly, "I couldn't bear to look at it, to see that python swallowing that tiny little bunny . . ."

In any event, she wasn't able to tell me anything about this question which interested me so much, and then finally, through a friend of a friend, who knew an authority on snakes, I found out what the scientific view of the issue was.

This specialist on snakes reported with disdainful certainty that no hypnosis was involved, that these are all legends that have come down to us from aboriginal savages (perhaps he had our natives in mind here?). In short, his pronouncement coincided completely with Ponderer's observations.

Deep down in my soul, I had always been sure that this was the case, but it was pleasant to hear a totally competent scientific confirmation of Ponderer's views. All the more so because the truly remarkable thinker's discoveries had been made long, long ago, when there still weren't any major scientific centers, no science to guide us and rule over us, as in our times, to define for us which snakes are useful and which are harmful, and why. Ponderer had to sacrifice his own skin to show us the correctness of his thinking.

By the way, I've noticed that some people get sad when they hear the story about the rabbits and boa constrictors. And others become upset and point out that the rabbits' situation wasn't all that bad, that they had quite a few interesting possibilities for making their lives better.

With all my inborn optimism (and putting my hand on the source of this optimism), I am compelled to say that in this case I like the person who finds this story gloomy more than the one who gets all excited and tries, perhaps, to influence the rabbits through the narrator.

Here's an illustrative example. You go to an acquaintance to borrow a bit of cash. As usual, you begin the conversation from far away — you talk about how hard it is to earn money, generally something like that. And so you see what effect this has.

If the person you're speaking with seizes on the topic and begins to get excited, showing you a multitude of ways in which money can be earned relatively easily, then you know he won't give you anything.

But if he starts to get gloomy while listening to your not very well-defined hints, and at the same time fails to point out ways of earning money fairly easily, then you know that things are going much better. This one might lend you the money, although he just as likely might not. But he's already gloomier, because in his mind he's already parted with his money, or if he's decided not to give you any, he's preparing himself to be stern and stubborn. Nevertheless, there is a chance.

Thus in the story about rabbits, I prefer the readers who are a bit sadder. It seems to me that I can expect greater benefit for the rabbits from them if indeed anything can help.